21 Yaks and a Speedo

How to Achieve Your Impossible

21 Yaks and a Speedo

How to Achieve Your Impossible

— Lewis Pugh —

Our Blue Future

London

Every effort has been made to trace copyright holders and to obtain their permission for the use of copyright material. The publishers apologise for any errors or omissions and would be grateful to be notified of any corrections that should be incorporated in future editions of this book.

All rights reserved.
No part of this publication may be reproduced or transmitted, in any form or by any means, without prior permission from the publisher or copyright holder.

© Lewis Pugh, 2013

® 'Speedo' is a registered trademark.

The moral right of the author has been asserted

Originally published in 2013 by

JONATHAN BALL PUBLISHERS (PTY) LTD
A division of Media24 (Pty) Ltd
PO Box 6836
Roggebaai, South Africa 8012

This edition published by
OUR BLUE FUTURE
75 Wells Street
London, UK
W1T 3QH

ISBN 978-0-620-57288-0

Also available as an eBook ISBN 978-0-620-57289-7

Cover design by Michiel Botha, Cape TownDesign and typesetting by Triple M Design, Johannesburg

Printed and bound by CPI Antony Rowe in the UK

To David Becker,
who inspired me to follow my own dreams

In accordance with the Official Secrets Act, the names of the soldiers of the British SAS, and the places in which they served, have been changed to protect their identity.

Contents

Introduction   1

Yak 1 – Channel   5
Yak 2 – *Vasbyt!*   19
Yak 3 – Escape   31
Yak 4 – Visualise   39
Yak 5 – Mind   51
Yak 6 – Blame   63
Yak 7 – Believe   75
Yak 8 – Push   89
Yak 9 – Follow   101
Yak 10 – Grind   115
Yak 11 – Test   127
Yak 12 – Open   141
Yak 13 – Hope   153
Yak 14 – Break   167
Yak 15 – Strive   183

Yak 16 – Plan	189
Yak 17 – Switch	201
Yak 18 – Trust	217
Yak 19 – Change	227
Yak 20 – Stand Up	239
Yak 21 – Dream	253
Timeline	265
Temperatures	269
Thanks	271

Introduction

I had never met a yak before I got to the Himalayas. We were on our way to Mount Everest to swim in a glacial lake, to draw attention to the impact of climate change on the Himalayan glaciers. And we had yaks to help us carry the heavy stuff.

During the two weeks it took us to get onto Mount Everest, I got to know those yaks. I trekked behind them up endless unforgiving slopes, watched them cross ridiculously thin bridges over sheer drops without changing their stride. I listened to them breathing outside my tent each night, and I witnessed their obstinacy each morning when our Sherpas tried to separate them from their feed bags and get them yoked up for a day's work.

I found myself thinking about the qualities of a yak, which got me imagining that these are not so different from the qualities people need to meet ordinary challenges (or extraordinary ones, for that matter). Focus. Tenacity. Obstinacy. I could relate to these.

I realised that they were not unlike the qualities and principles I've relied on during my many swims and expeditions, key principles that have enabled me to push my personal limits and achieve things people assured me were impossible.

Some of these are qualities I found and developed in myself. Others are lessons and strategies I've learned along the way from fellow swimmers and other athletes, from soldiers and farmers and mountaineers, from fishermen and CEOs, from shipowners and kayakers, from billionaires and lighthouse keepers.

In talking to people around the world, whether individually or in large auditoriums, I have learned that these principles resonate with people in business, in sport, in their personal lives, in whatever endeavour they take on, whatever challenges they face.

Every expedition requires something different

Introduction

in terms of crew, equipment and planning. Many, many people play a role in my expeditions, and they are acknowledged at the back of the book. But I want to collectively thank them here, because if there is one thing that has enabled me to do what I've been able to do, it's my team.

There are 21 stories here, each one corresponding to an expedition that we have undertaken, and each one illustrating a principle we've come to rely on. I've called them 'yaks', after those strong, stubborn beasts that never gave up and almost never complained. The principles themselves are simple, but effective. Stick by them, and they'll see you through. Just like a yak.

— Yak 1 —

Channel

Channel your energies and focus forward. If the desire is deep enough, you'll get it done.

Every endurance swimmer wants to swim the English Channel. It's the Everest of swims, not because it's the most difficult, but because it's the one against which every other swim is measured.

I was just 23 years old when I stood on the white cliffs of Dover and looked out over that historic piece of water, knowing I was going to attempt to reach the other side in nothing but a Speedo swimming costume, a cap and goggles. I had a few swims under my belt. I'd done two Robben Island swims, and swum across Lake Malawi with my swimming buddy and mentor, Otto Thaning.

My father had been sick in hospital for a number of years when I met Otto at the Sea Point swimming pool. He was a heart surgeon who had trained under Dr Christiaan Barnard, and he had the most technically beautiful swimming stroke I had ever seen. Otto knew how I dreamed of doing this swim, so he invited me to come to Dover and attempt the crossing with him.

The first thing we did when we arrived at Dover was run up the cliffs to Dover Castle and look out over the English Channel. Below was the busy harbour, with its ferries and hovercrafts and container ships, and way over on the other side were the white cliffs of France. William the Conqueror crossed near here. Both Napoleon and Hitler contemplated an invasion by sea. This historic piece of water divided Britain from Europe – and I desperately wanted to swim across it.

Endurance swimming is unique. If you want to run the London Marathon, you know exactly when it is going to take place. You know exactly where it's going to start and finish. You know that when you arrive at Greenwich there will be organisers at the ready, there will be marshals there to help, there will be drink stations every kilometre, and if anything goes wrong there will be paramedics and people to look after you.

Channel

It's very different when you arrive at the English Channel, because you have to organise it all yourself. We'd found a boat and a pilot – a fisherman named Richard Armstrong who supplemented his income by doing Channel crossings. Now we had to decide which day to go.

We met Richard as soon as we arrived, and he told us that the conditions were looking good for the very next day. 'It's going to start out a bit choppy,' he said, 'but it will flatten out later on, so I really think one of you should go for it. Some people arrive here and wait three weeks for a decent day.'

The boat could follow only one swimmer at a time, so we needed to make a choice. Otto was a much better swimmer than me. If he went first and didn't make it, it would have a terrible psychological impact on me. So I asked him if I could try first. He generously agreed.

I went straight out and bought a tub of 'Channel Grease' at Boots. (Much later, when we did the swims in the polar regions, we realised that lathering this thick, lardy stuff all over you doesn't make a jot of difference to the cold, but nobody ever questioned its efficacy!) We were leaving from Shakespeare Beach at 4am, so I also stocked up on bananas, chocolate and energy drinks, and then turned in for the evening. It seemed that my head had hardly touched the pillow when the alarm woke me up at 2am. This was it!

Peter Bales had come from Cape Town to be our seconder. He'd swum the Channel before, and was well equipped to provide food, water and moral support during the swim. Otto wished us luck, and we set off to find Richard on his fishing boat. He offloaded crates and fishing nets in the dark to make space for us. Someone from the Channel Swimming Association would join us, to make the swim official.

The Association rules are simple: you start on dry land, you finish on dry land; you are not allowed to hold onto the boat to eat or drink or rest; and you may wear only a

> *'The Association rules are simple: you start on dry land, you finish on dry land.'*

Speedo swimming costume, cap and goggles, and as much grease as takes your fancy.

When we cast off I could see the waves crashing off the harbour wall. As we reached open water they started surging over the front of the boat. I can still remember the booming sound as the waves slammed the hull. I gave Peter a look that said, 'Have we done the right thing?'

'Trust your pilot,' he told me.

I was about to learn endurance swimming lesson number one: when you swim from England to France you've got to leave your doubt on the beach at Dover.

> *'When you swim from England to France you've got to leave your doubt on the beach at Dover.'*

My plan was not to rush this swim. It wasn't a race, and I just wanted to make it across. From the moment I got in the water, I told myself, I would try to relax. But there was no chance of that.

The first hour was like being in a washing machine. I often got a mouthful of seawater or was whacked by a wave and thrown backwards. It

Yak 1

stayed that way for the second hour, and the third, and the fourth. The sun was up by then and I kept looking back over my shoulder, but the big white cliffs never seemed to retreat. 'Don't look back, that's not the direction in which you're going,' Peter shouted.

After five hours I started thinking I wasn't going to make it. Quitting is a dangerous thing to do, because it can easily become a habit. I know too many swimmers who quit when the going gets tough. But that makes it doubly difficult when you come back to try it again, because you have to get over the mental hurdle of not having made it the first time.

Most people give up at the proverbial eleventh hour. But here's endurance swimming lesson number two: when you stand on Shakespeare Beach about to dive into the sea, you are already halfway to France. That's because all the training you did to get there, all the organising and fundraising, is also part of the effort.

> *'Quitting is a dangerous thing to do, because it can easily become a habit.'*

That's what I kept telling myself. And gradually, between the fifth and the sixth hour, the sea miraculously flattened out. It became like a millpond; there was not a ripple on the water. But I was already exhausted. Sometime during the tenth hour I heard Peter say, 'Two hours to go!' At least, that's what I thought I heard. So I put in a really good fast hour. When I put my head up again, I expected to hear that I only had one hour left, but Peter told me I still had *four* hours to go. I couldn't believe it!

Occasionally I stopped to have a bit of banana and some energy drink, treading water all the while. The food was mixing with the seawater in my stomach, and it felt like there was a volcano in there. Vomiting and swimming are not mutually compatible activities, but this was out of my control. All I could do was try to get the angle just right.

Peter was watching me retch and tread water, and he started to giggle. It was the best thing he could have done, because I was starting to feel sorry for myself. For the next hour I kept putting my head up to see how far we had to go. 'I promise you, Lewis,' Peter said, 'I will be the first to tell you when you're nearly there. Just keep on going.'

About an hour off the coast of France, a new urgency came into Peter's voice. The tide was turning. 'You've got to swim hard now, Lewis!' he shouted. 'If we miss Cap Gris Nez over there you'll be swept down the coast and that will add on another five hours to your swim.' *Another five hours?*

If you run the London Marathon, you know that you are going to be running 42.2km. You know where the start is, and it would be a huge surprise to you if, when you arrived in The Mall for the final kilometre of the marathon, the organisers told you the finish had been moved to the top of Primrose Hill in Regent's Park, some five kilometres away. But that's the unpredictability of endurance swimming.

I stuck my head down and swam as fast as I could. Everyone was spurring me on now. Richard had left the wheelhouse, and was leaning over the gunwale shouting, 'C'mon, son!'

And then I heard the sweetest sound – the lap

of ripples on the shore. I could see the pale golden sand beneath me, and if I'd had more strength I would have dived down to touch it. Just a few more strokes, and then that glorious feeling of putting my feet on French sand. I fell onto the beach and kissed the ground.

Here's another way that swimming is different from running a marathon: there are no crowds there to cheer you at the finish. There was a lone fisherman 200m away. He looked at me collapsed on the sand, and then threw his line back into the sea.

My overwhelming emotion was relief. The swim had taken me 14 hours and 50 minutes. But there was no time for quiet reflection; the crew were keen to get back to England to start Otto's swim while the weather was still good, and that would take us another four hours.

I've seconded a number of Channel swims since that day, and developed four essential rules. One, find an experienced pilot who can find you the shortest distance across. Two, have patience – people get frustrated and pick the wrong day to cross, but timing is everything. Three, do your cold-water training – 18°C feels icy after 15 or 20 hours. And four, have someone really inspiring on your boat who can make good judgment calls. They need to keep you going as long as you can, and get you out as soon as you can't.

Gruelling as it was, when I look back now I know everything lined up perfectly for me on that swim. Because if you get any one of those four rules badly wrong, you can be Michael Phelps and you still won't make it across the Channel.

We arrived back to the lights of Dover Castle twinkling. I was famished and, after eating bananas and chocolate for 15 hours, was fantasising about a chicken burger. But by the time I'd walked the kilometre back to the hotel, wrapped in a blanket and slathered in Channel Grease, it was 11pm and the bar had closed. There was no room service in the hotel, so I grabbed a handful of discarded peanuts at the bar to tide me over until breakfast.

That swim powered me through so many things later in life. When people say to me, you must have the strongest mind in the world to swim across the

North Pole, or off Antarctica or on Mount Everest, I tell them that endurance swimming builds good mental strength.

I don't know of any sport where the goalposts can shift the way they do with endurance swimming. You can expect the English Channel swim to take 12 hours – as I did – and find yourself swimming for another three hours before you finally reach the other side. (As I did.)

> *'I don't know of any sport where the goalposts can shift the way they do with endurance swimming.'*

The English Channel was my first big swim, and it set me up for all the rest that would follow. And it taught me the most important endurance swimming lesson of all: if you just keep on going, one stroke at a time, eventually you *will* reach France.

— Yak 2 —

Vasbyt!

If at first you don't succeed … persevere until you do.

It's impossible to describe what it feels like to be left on the mountain to die, but it's a moment you never forget. I was lying on an exposed slope with a busted knee on the wildest, wettest Welsh night in living memory. The sleet was coming in sideways. It was freezing cold, and my colleagues on the final test of the Special Air Service (SAS) selection course had just abandoned me to my fate. As I watched their backs disappear into the black night I wanted to curse them, but I was too exhausted.

The Afrikaans word *vasbyt* is so expressive, and we don't have an equivalent in the English language. It means bite down hard. Don't quit. Keep on going! And because of the physical nature of what I do I've had plenty of moments where I've had to *vasbyt*. But that gruelling final

— Yak 2 —

run on the SAS Test Week is the one I remember most vividly.

My father was a military man, and I had dreamed of serving in the British Army ever since I was a young boy. But even before I ended up sheltering in that ditch, my prospects had not looked good. The SAS selection course is tough; on my first attempt, I failed to make the 24-hour cut-off time on the very last day after sustaining a knee injury, and I got very sick on the second try. Now I was over 30 years old, and I had been given a third chance. I was, to my knowledge, the first person in 60 years to be given such an opportunity to become an SAS reservist. So I knew this attempt really would be my last.

The final day of Test Week took place in the Brecon Beacons in Wales. It was an 80km run over marshy and mountainous terrain, carrying over 30kg on your back and a rifle in your hand. It's called Endurance – for good reason. The cut-off time was 24 hours. It sounds tough enough, but it also came after a week of non-stop running and just a few hours of sleep. We had started the week with over 100 recruits, and less than half remained. This night they would drop like ninepins.

My feet were badly blistered and I had been struggling all week with my right knee. Add to that the appalling weather conditions. It was midwinter and the rain that week had been the heaviest locals could remember. There were observers from a Scandinavian Special Forces unit with us who said it was the coldest night they had ever experienced. When soldiers from that part of the world tell you that, you know it's cold! It was a wet cold, with pouring rain, howling wind, and driving sleet and snow. The wind chill makes it feel much colder than the dry Arctic cold. And rumours that the training staff might cancel Endurance due to the severity of the weather proved to be unfounded.

This was not my first time in the Brecon Beacons. Besides the fact that I'd attempted the course twice before, I had spent many pleasant days hik-

'We had started the week with over 100 recruits, and less than half remained. This night they would drop like ninepins.'

ing there. I had family in the area (my parents are both Welsh), and just a few months earlier my mother had come out from South Africa for a visit. We'd spent some wonderful days in the nearby Erwood Valley watching chestnut-coloured red kites, recently brought back from the brink of extinction, soaring above us. We had marvelled at the beauty of the place and at the resilience of the environment and its species when proper measures are taken to protect them.

The mountains were a very different place the night of Endurance. At 5pm we were over halfway through the route, and time was of the essence. It was getting dark fast and the snow and the sleet were driving into our faces. However, because I was familiar with the area, I knew some sheep tracks for getting around some of the more difficult parts, and was able to save valuable time. I was with about eight other recruits at this point, and more than once they thanked me for getting them through the boggy spots.

We'd just made it to the summit of Cadair Berwyn and begun our descent to Lake Gwyn when my knee suddenly gave out. I'd been managing it with a combination of anti-inflammatories and painkillers. But when I felt it buckle underneath me I knew I was in deep trouble. Even through the analgesics, it felt as if someone had driven a six-inch nail through the outside of my right leg. 'Guys,' I screamed, 'my knee has gone! Give me a minute to get some food and painkillers into me.'

Now, the instructions we'd been given at the beginning of Test Week were clear: if one of your fellow recruits goes down, you stop and make sure they're OK before you move on and get help. Put up a bivouac, get some food into them – but do not leave them until they are 100% safe. Hypothermia has killed more than a few SAS recruits over the years. Any time spent helping a colleague would be subtracted from your finishing time, so there would be no penalty. As my exhausted comrades contemplated my situation, I could see the cogs moving in their collective brain. They were desperately tired, and worried about the time limit. Hypothermia might also have muddled their thinking. 'Sorry, pal,' a Scottish recruit eventually spoke for all of them. 'We can't afford to wait in this storm.' So much for the buddy who had guided them around the bogs and showed them the short cuts. I had just become a burden, and I was being abandoned.

'As I watched them disappear into the dark night, the terror came over me ... I was in a life-or-death situation.'

As I watched them disappear into the dark night, the terror came over me. I had been left on the side of the mountain in freezing conditions. Snow had already begun building up around me. The last rendezvous point was a kilometre back up the mountain, and no one would be able to hear my calls for help above the noise of the storm. I was not sure I had the strength even to crawl back up the mountain. I was in a life-or-death situation.

I crawled into a ditch for shelter and took some food and some painkillers. The combination of sheer exhaustion and the cold made me drowsy, and I fought the urge to sleep. In those conditions, once you lie down it is very difficult to get up and get going again. Hypothermia was threatening,

Vasbyt!

and that would be the end of me. My choice was stark and simple: move or die.

That cold realisation was like a shot of adrenaline. I managed to lever myself upwards, used my weapon as a walking stick (a punishable offence, but what choice did I have?) and continued down the mountain.

I still had 25km to go, and I knew I was now well behind time. It took me over an hour and a half to stumble and slide down that mountain. I fell on the icy path dozens of times; I just had to get up and carry on. In the SAS the instructors always say: 'Self-pity is a weak man's emotion.' They are not wrong. When you start feeling sorry for yourself, it's all over.

'When you start feeling sorry for yourself, it's all over.'

Once I was off the mountain, I still had another eight hours to go, including the infamous VW (Voluntary Withdrawal) Valley – so called because so many recruits have given up in it. But some words of encouragement from an officer at the rendezvous point spurred me on. Eventually I caught up with some of the recruits who had left me behind. One of them had already succumbed to hypothermia and had dropped out. Of the original eight, only one would make it to the end. I didn't know this then, as I continued on, alone.

The temptation to give up was there throughout those last gruelling kilometres. But I remembered what Winston Churchill famously said: 'If you are going through hell, keep going.' So I made a deal with myself. Whenever I thought of quitting, I would just ask myself a simple question: 'Lewis, can you take just one more step?' If the answer was yes, then I would take it.

> *'Whenever I thought of quitting, I would just ask myself a simple question: "Lewis, can you take just one more step?" If the answer was yes, then I would take it.'*

I asked myself that question many times. And each time I took that next step, swinging my damaged right leg stiffly along beside me. 'You cut that fine, Pugh!' the Training Officer said when I crossed the finish line. 'Twenty-three hours and 58

Vasbyt!

minutes.' I'd made it, just two minutes before the final cut-off time.

I've returned to that course in my mind many times over the years. It was the first time I experienced how powerful the mind can be when focused on a goal. As Nietzsche said, if you have a *why* you can bear almost any *how*. I had my why in my long-held dream of serving in the British Special Forces. That dream gave me the strength to withstand the how, to grit my teeth, to *vasbyt*, and to keep on going.

When you come to the end of your resources, when you feel utterly beaten and exhausted, ask yourself, 'Can I take just one more step?' If the answer is yes, take it. As sure as the sun will rise in the morning, you *will* get through the challenge, one way or another. And you'll have the rest of your days to remember how you did it.

— Yak 3 —

Escape

Sometimes escape is not an option. It's a necessity.

The selection course for the SAS lasts over a year. It ends, for the lucky few who make it that far, with an interrogation phase.

Now, the entire course is intensely challenging, but this last phase ... well, to put it mildly, it's robust! This is where they test whether you can withstand a forceful interrogation should you be captured by the enemy. I don't know for how long the interrogation went on, but it was exhausting. It really felt as if they had kept the 'best' for last.

At the end of it, we were driven to a lonely Welsh beach. It was long and barren and windswept, and as we stood there on the sand the realisation slowly seeped in. We had done it. We had survived the most gruelling training imaginable. We had made it through.

Our thoughts were interrupted by the drone

of engines. An enormous Hercules transport plane landed on the beach in front of us and taxied to a stop. Out of it stepped the commanding officer of the SAS. It was the first time any of us had met him.

We saluted him as he walked up to us, and he told us to stand at ease while he addressed us. 'Gentlemen,' he said, 'I'm very proud of you today and I want to tell you two things.'

'I am proud that you had the grit and determination to carry on.' We felt proud too. Over 200 people from my squadron had started the training, and just three of us had passed. On that day we were to receive our sand-coloured beret with the badge with the winged dagger and the motto, 'Who Dares Wins'. 'But I want you to appreciate that at the end of the day, we are just ordinary infantry soldiers. The only difference between us and the other Special Forces units in the world,' he said, 'is that we do the basics better than anybody else.'

'If you get the basics right, everything else falls into place.'

That really struck me, because it's a great principle to live by. If you get the basics right, everything else falls into place. I've seen this repeatedly in life, whenever I've met outstanding people. Whether they were athletes or lawyers, soldiers or businesspeople, they paid attention to the basics.

But it was the next thing the commanding officer said that really struck me. 'You have just come off the interrogation phase,' he continued. 'It's not outside the realms of possibility that one day you might get captured. Wherever that might be, if you are captured you have a duty as an SAS soldier to attempt to escape. At every moment and every opportunity that arises, you must attempt to escape. An escaped soldier ties up lots of enemy personnel and it enables the rest of us to finish the job. We also need you back to help us with the fight.'

Then came the clincher. 'And if you fail to take that opportunity,' he went on, 'at the end of the war, when the International Committee of the Red Cross hands you over and you are brought back to British soil, I will find out. And I will charge you and I will make sure you also serve time in a Brit-

— Yak 3 —

ish jail. That's how seriously we take this duty.'

Now, this was a time when I was working as a lawyer in London, and it also seemed to be to be the best advice you could give a trainee solicitor, or any other young professional for that matter. It's so simple. Do your training, but if you find that you do not enjoy the work, you have a duty to escape while you can. If you don't, you will be a prisoner for the rest of your life. Your prison will be self-imposed, and you will have only yourself to blame for it.

> *'If you do not enjoy your work, you have a duty to escape while you can. If you don't, you will be a prisoner for the rest of your life.'*

I know so many people who didn't escape when they had the opportunity. And now they have responsibilities – careers and marriages and children and mortgages – and they feel as if they've missed their chance.

But I thought about something else our commanding officer said that day: *there will always be an opportunity to escape*. The best chance usually

Escape

comes near the beginning of your capture, when there is chaos all around. Escape is much more difficult once you've been taken back to a base, or a prisoner of war camp with guards and cameras all around you.

The same thing applies to a lawyer or an accountant who feels trapped in their job. Don't wait until you are 45 years old to realise you don't really want to be an accountant. The warning signs were there all along – the lack of enthusiasm, that feeling every Sunday afternoon knowing that, next day, you have to go back to a job you don't enjoy.

The point is, chances to escape come more than once in a lifetime. Don't live to regret the fact that you didn't escape when you could. Don't look back on a wasted opportunity, or perhaps even a wasted life. Don't pause when it's too late and wonder whether you could have been or done so much more. Take action. Now.

> *'Chances to escape come more than once in a lifetime. Don't live to regret the fact that you didn't escape when you could.'*

— Yak 3 —

Make no mistake, it takes courage to make a big escape. You'll be going into the unknown. It also takes sacrifice – even if the thing you are giving up is nothing more than your comfort zone.

But here's the rub: I've met plenty of people who have followed their dreams. And not a single one of them regrets doing so.

— Yak 4 —

Visualise

If you can see it in your mind's eye, you can make it happen.

Penguins are my favourite sea birds, but puffins come a close second. The most amazing thing about puffins is the way they fly. It's just wonderfully frenetic.

I will never forget my first visit to Norway's North Cape, which coincided with the puffins' seasonal migration. The Norwegians say you can set your watch by their arrival, and on the day I set out to do a recce of my North Cape swim, the puffins were there *en masse*. With their orange beaks and their black and white harlequin faces, they flapped like mad through the air and through the water. There were thousands of them, diving in and surging out again, all around our boat. To witness that was something special. And the puffins became a key part of my visualisation for that crucial swim – the first long-distance swim ever attempted within the Arctic Circle.

— Yak 4 —

More than any other swim before or since, the North Cape swim taught me the power of visualisation. Visualisation closes the gap between where you are and where you need to be.

> *'Visualisation closes the gap between where you are and where you need to be.'*

The idea for my North Cape swim began long before I had ever been to Norway. I was working in London, and at the same time also serving as a reservist in the SAS. I hadn't swum for a few years, and I missed it. I love swimming. I love the action of swimming, I love the feeling of diving into cold water, and getting out invigorated and refreshed. But every weekend and every holiday I was in the SAS running and diving into ditches and climbing up mountains, and I really missed the ocean.

So I decided it was time to do a swim. I opened up an atlas and began to trace some of my previous swims. One of them had been around the southernmost point of Africa, and I thought to myself: why don't I try to do the most northerly point of mainland Europe? And there it was: the North Cape.

Visualise

It's got such a stark name, and I suspected it might be too cold to swim there. But I decided to go and take a look.

So I flew from London to Oslo and from Oslo to Tromsø, from Tromsø to Hammerfest and from Hammerfest to Honningsvåg, a picturesque little fishing village of about 2,500 people. From there I took a tourist bus to the North Cape.

I had seen the North Cape in photographs, but nothing prepared me for the spectacular beauty of the place.

Because I've been to all the world's oceans, people always ask me which is the most beautiful cape in the world. It's almost like asking a parent which child they love the most; it's difficult, because each is unique and each is special. I do some of my training off the Cape of Good Hope at the southern tip of Africa – the one Sir Francis Drake called the 'Fairest Cape in All

'People always ask me which is the most beautiful cape in the world. It's almost like asking a parent which child they love the most.'

the World'. That said, Norway's North Cape is just astonishingly beautiful.

Maybe it's the latitude. At 71°N you really do feel that you are at the end of the world; between there and the North Pole is virtually nothing but water and ice. Or maybe it had something to do with the light. Photographers love the first and the last half-hours of the day; the light is perfect and that's when you get the magical shot. The light at the North Cape is like that all day long. In summer, it's 24 hours of sunlight. In winter, of course, it's 24 hours of darkness. But in summer, other than at midday, you have this glorious, pale light.

It was cold outside, about 5°C and bracing. I walked up to the edge of the cliff, and there was a sheer drop of 300m down to the ocean. Along the edge of the cliff there were grazing reindeer, with their wonderful soft grey coats and dark forked antlers. The scene was worlds away from my life as a London lawyer. I decided right then and there: I want to go for this.

But first I needed a boat and a pilot. The tourist office in Honningsvåg told me that the person to

Visualise

speak to was Hugo Salamonsen, and that I would either find him at the harbour or in the Bryggerie, a local pub. So I walked down the street, past blue and red and yellow fishermen's houses. I found Hugo in the pub, and I heard him before I saw him; he had the heartiest laugh in all the world. He also had earrings in each ear and looked a little bit like a pirate.

Within five minutes of chatting to Hugo, I knew he was the man for the job. I had one last question for him: could I do it? He didn't dismiss me, and he didn't raise my hopes either. 'Nobody has ever swum around the North Cape before,' he said. 'I don't know how good a swimmer you are, but you will definitely need the right day.'

I had to be back at work in London the next day. At the airport, I bought a Norwegian flag. I hung it above my bed, along with the photographs I had taken from the cliff top. My visualisation had begun.

The next few months were punishing. Two or three times a week I travelled from London to Dover by bus to do my swimming. On the weekends was SAS training; the Iraq War had just broken out and we were on standby. I was lean and fit, because at any moment we could be running through the desert with heavy equipment on our backs, but this wasn't the ideal physical state for a cold-water swim. I'd been told to expect water temperatures of as low as 4°C in August off the North Cape, and I weighed just 85kg. (By comparison, when I swam the North Pole four years later I was a much more insulated 105kg.)

Every morning when I woke up I would see that Norwegian flag, and I would say to myself: *you're going to be there very soon*. I'd put on my suit and tie and look at the photographs on my wardrobe and tell myself, *just do the training, you're going to be swimming around North Cape soon*.

The big moment arrived, and it was back to Honningsvåg. I'd brought my SAS buddy Nick Peterson along to be my seconder. Nick had been my SAS instructor, and he is also a lawyer. At the North Cape, we were entering dangerous waters. Nobody had ever swum here before. This was a world away from the English Channel and Robben Island. Nick and I met up with Hugo to map the route by water in his Zodiac. That was the day

Visualise

we met the puffin migration, and that was when the serious visualisation began. Hugo took us on a slow ride along the 5km route, which gave me the opportunity to mentally imprint the landscape, so that I could completely visualise the swim from beginning to end in my mind's eye. I took in every single rock, the crags on the cliff face, even the distinguishing marks from sea-bird droppings.

The recce took about 30 minutes (the swim itself would take an hour and four minutes). As we came to the end point, at a little bay called Hornvika, the final piece of the jigsaw puzzle fell into place. That was the moment I realised I could do this swim.

In the days to come, while we waited for the right conditions, I replayed the swim over and over in my mind. I used all my senses for the visualisation. In addition to seeing the intricate details of the landscape, I listened to the putt-putt-putt of the boat's engine, and to the noise of the puffins and the seagulls and the sound of the waves crashing up against the cliffs. I smelled the fresh air just in from the high Arctic, and felt the icy-cold water over my body as I dived in. I imagined the nervous dry taste I get in my mouth just before a swim, and the way it would be relieved by the wet taste of salt water.

We were still worried about the end. Hornvika Bay is surrounded by 300m cliffs, so there is no way to get a helicopter or an ambulance in there. If something went wrong, it would be a long boat drive to get me back to safety. We needed a way to warm me up. The beach was filled with driftwood, and we decided we could use this to build a bonfire. That bonfire became a key part of my visualisation, as I imagined myself standing near the flames at the end of the swim. I threw in a few grazing reindeer too, for good measure.

Two days later, we got the perfect conditions. Still, I was nervous; this would be the first time a long-distance swim had ever been done above the Arctic Circle. But as we were preparing the boat, Hugo walked up to me and changed everything. 'Lewis, I'm so proud of you,' he said. Such a simple compliment, from somebody I hardly knew. And I thought, 'I'm going to do this for you, Hugo.'

Visualise

I dived in and went for it. I passed all the landmarks, and knew where I was at 20 minutes, and at 30 minutes. Then, at 50 minutes, I got a massive cramp. I was really feeling the cold, but I had to stop and stretch my foot. To carry on required a delicate balance: too fast and I got cramp, too slow and I wouldn't generate enough body heat. As I entered the bay, with 400m to go, I put my head up and couldn't believe what I saw. The flames of a massive bonfire lit up the rock face, and the smoke was rising right to the top of the cliffs. I just had to get to that fire!

So I did. Sitting on a piece of driftwood, thawing next to the flames, I looked out and saw reindeer grazing on the grassy verge of the beach. Then one of the Sami herdsmen came up to me, the bells on his traditional hat jingling, and offered me a mug of warm reindeer blood. I politely took a sip and passed it on. That drink was the only thing I hadn't visualised – everything else was exactly right, down to the last reindeer.

After I'd warmed up, Nick and I walked up to the top of the cliff. We sat there and looked out

Yak 4

> *'Thoughts alone won't make extraordinary things happen. But nothing ever happens if you don't visualise it first.'*

towards the North Pole. And we both knew what we were thinking.

Thoughts alone won't make extraordinary things happen. But nothing ever happens if you don't visualise it first.

— Yak 5 —

Mind

Thoughts are so powerful. How often do you think about what you are thinking about?

My best friend David Becker always says to me: 'Lewis, if you think you are going to get cold in the sea, you will.' You often get what you expect in life. So it's vitally important to think about what you are thinking about.

I remember exactly what I was thinking about when I swam across Magdalenefjord in Spitsbergen, the largest island in the Svalbard archipelago, in 2005. I was thinking about history. At 79°N, it was the most northerly long-distance swim ever undertaken.

Spitsbergen is about 1,000km from the North Pole, and the water temperature there averages 4°C – even at the height of summer, when the sun shines for 24 hours. Although I had swum the length of Norway's Sognefjord the year before in water that sometimes went as low as 6°C, I knew

> *'I knew that two degrees lower was another world. Get it wrong and you will end up hypothermic. Or worse.'*

that two degrees lower was another world. Get it wrong and you *will* end up hypothermic. Or worse.

The thing about doing something for the first time is that you don't have medical or anecdotal statistics at hand to tell you that it can be done. On the contrary, all I had to go on was stories of the Arctic convoys that resupplied the Soviet Union during the Second World War. My father was a surgeon in the Royal Navy, and I remembered the stories he told me about the American and British convoys that braved German U-boats and land-based aircraft to get supplies to the Russian ports of Murmansk and Arkhangelsk. If a ship was hit, the sailors had mere minutes in the water before they became too cold to swim and sank straight to the bottom.

Needless to say, I trained for that swim like never before. And during that training I discovered something new. Determined people talk about 'mind over matter'; while training for that swim,

Mind

I discovered that mind and matter can work together to do something quite extraordinary.

I trained in Cape Town with renowned sports scientist Professor Tim Noakes and his assistant Dr Jonathan Dugas. This was my first swim with the Prof (many more would follow), and, as much as I would be putting my life on the line, he was putting his professional reputation in my hands. If something went wrong on this swim, fingers would point at him. There was a lot at stake.

Finding water cold enough to train in was our first challenge. If you've ever jumped into the surf off Camps Bay Beach, you know how cold the sea off Africa's southern tip can be. But it was nowhere near cold enough to prepare me for swimming in the Arctic Ocean.

We tried adding ice to a friend's swimming pool, but it melted almost immediately and made little difference to the water temperature. That's when I called my friend Motti Lewis. As a wine maker, he knows a good deal about the winemaking process, which involves cooling the wine to very low temperatures. Motti did some calculations to work out exactly how much ice we would need to chill the pool. We quickly realised that an ordinary garden swimming pool was not going to work, so we bought a small portable pool. Motti measured the volume, did some calculations, and worked out that we would need about one and a half tons of ice to get the water temperature down to 3°C. That's enough ice to fill a minivan! Where to find such a steady supply of ice? Not in your local corner shop.

We found it at the V&A Waterfront. We set up our pool in the deepwater trawling division of I&J, where the fishing trawlers dock when they come in from the South Atlantic. Those ships need tons of ice to keep their fish fresh, and I&J was kind enough to let us have the use of their ice-making machines.

We trained there every afternoon. When we arrived, a forklift truck would deliver huge bucketloads of ice to our pool. We also needed help getting the ice into the pool; for some reason, we were never short of volunteers, as the fisherman lined up to help shovel ice onto this crazy guy in the blue Portapool.

Inside the pool, we had rigged a harness that held me in place while I swam – a sort of aquatic version of a stationary bike. Every day I would cover a kilometre. And every day we would bring the temperature down by one degree. We did this until we got the temperature down to 5°C. And then something happened.

> *'Inside the pool, we had rigged a harness that held me in place while I swam – a sort of aquatic version of a stationary bike.'*

Dropping from 6°C to 5°C, the pain ratchets up incredibly. Every degree further down you go, I would discover, you really feel the difference. But right then and there, I couldn't get into the water.

Working with Jonathan was a case of right person, right place, right time. Jonathan's father was in the US Air Force, and Jonathan had grown up on a number of US military bases, so he was used to being around a certain kind of lingo. While we were training he often took on the tone of a drill sergeant. This gave me an idea.

'Let's try something different,' I said to Jonathan that day, while I was trying to psyche myself up to jump in. I asked him to mimic the countdown that the Royal Air Force dispatcher gives paratroopers in the moments right before they leap out of the plane.

Here's the thing you need to know about my parachute jumps during my time with SAS: I was never a good jumper, but I turned into a terrified jumper when one jump went horribly wrong. It was a night jump, and there were 30 of us crammed like sardines in the back of a Hercules, lined up and ready to jump out of the plane's port and starboard doors. The RAF dispatchers always tried to get us out evenly, and there was usually about a second between jumps.

It was a dark night, and after we took off we flew through some rain. As I was about to jump, the trooper in front of me slipped and somehow got caught, half in and half out of the plane. I saw the panic on his face, and I remember him screaming and the RAF dispatcher desperately trying to get him out of the plane. The only way was by kicking him. He was stuck there and his helmet was being

Mind

beaten against the side of the aeroplane – and then he was gone. And I had to follow.

A parachute jump for the SAS is very different from a civilian jump; you can't really steer a British Army parachute, and with all the equipment you are carrying you land fast and hard, which is why they say a good jump is one you walk away from. After I landed I discarded my parachute, and found that my inner layer of clothing was so wet with sweat that I could have wrung it out like a flannel. That's when I realised how scared I had been. Every time I jumped after that was terrifying for me. When you see something go wrong, it's hard to get it out of your mind. So instead of shuffling towards the exit door like the rest of the guys, I had to get really aggressive and launch myself out of the plane with sheer determination.

> *'When you see something go wrong, it's hard to get it out of your mind.'*

That was the emotion I drew on when I had to overcome my aversion to the 5°C water. 'Just work with me on this one,' I told Jonathan, who by this time was no longer just a scientist but also an instructor, safety supervisor and coach. And he took on the RAF dispatcher role with gusto. I described the red-amber-green traffic lights that told the paratroopers when to jump, and the way the dispatcher would count down, 'Red on, GREEN ON – GO! GO! GO!'

I told him I was going to close my eyes and imagine that I was there. He would do the commands, and I would dive into the pool on cue. Jonathan did that countdown better than any RAF dispatcher. I jumped in and swam the kilometre and jumped out. I hadn't felt a thing.

Professor Tim Noakes was astounded: my body temperature had *risen* to 38.4°C! Now, normal is 37°C, so going up 1.4° doesn't sound like a lot, but there is a very narrow range in human thermoregulation; go down 2° and you're clinically hypothermic; up 2° and you're hyperthermic. 'I can't believe what I'm seeing, Lewis,' the Prof said. 'It's like you've created this heat before you got in the water.' He coined the term 'anticipatory thermogenesis' to describe this process. We now had hard

Mind

evidence of how the power of thought can actually create a physiological change in our bodies.

The Magdalenefjord swim went off without a hitch. In fact, it was the perfect swim. Spitsbergen is one of the most breathtakingly beautiful places on earth. A massive turquoise glacier feeds into Magdalenefjord, with chunks of ice as big as buildings breaking off and landing in the water to float away as icebergs.

As I swam past them, with my head in the water, I heard a tantalising sound: a snap-crackle-pop, just like Rice Krispies in milk. It was the sound of tiny air bubbles being released from the ice – air that had been trapped there as much as 3,000 years ago. To swim through this sound, I thought, is to swim in history.

Some of that oxygen must have gone to my head; even though I had broken the record by swimming at 79°N, I decided that a swim at 80°N sounded even more tantalising. That would be just ten degrees away from the North Pole. There was a roundness to that figure that I liked.

Twelve hours later, having just warmed up, I

— Yak 5 —

was standing on a desolate beach at the northernmost point of Spitsbergen ready to dive into the Arctic Ocean again. What on earth was I thinking?

'If you can swim through history, you can make history. You just have to put your mind to it.'

I'll tell you what I was thinking: if you can swim through history, you can make history. You just have to put your mind to it.

— Yak 6 —

Blame

Blame no one but yourself.

Nothing prepares you for the bloodcurdling sound of a leopard seal. Some animals look cute, even though you know they're dangerous. Look at polar bears – you just want to cuddle them. Even hippos – I always want to tug those beautiful little ears. But not leopard seals.

A leopard seal will be lying there on the Antarctic sea ice and it will raise its head and look at you and you think it's going to grunt or perhaps bark. But instead it will hiss. The sound is like a monitor lizard, or some kind of poisonous beast.

Leopard seals are big – easily 3m long – and can weigh up to 600kg. Their jaws are huge and can open to 160° – like those of a moray eel. Their soft grey coats are covered in dark spots. They have round eyes like a doll's – and a split personality. One moment they're your best mate, and next they

> *'One moment they're your best mate, and next they are trying to drag you down to the bottom of the sea to drown you. It's just astonishing.'*

are trying to drag you down to the bottom of the sea to drown you. One moment they've grabbed an Adélie penguin (among my favourite creatures in the world), shaken it to death and delivered it to your feet as a gift, the next they are at your throat trying to rip it apart. It's just astonishing.

So you can understand why leopard seals were on my mind in 2005 when we took a full scientific team down to Antarctica to document what would happen to my body during the southernmost swim ever undertaken. We chose Petermann Island in the Antarctic Peninsula, at latitude 65°S, as our venue. Which just happened to be a favourite playground for leopard seals.

At the North Pole (in 2007) we would have Russian polar bear guards (armed, but under strict instructions not to harm any bears). In Antarctica we had Dr Damon Stanwell-Smith as our safety watch during the swim. Damon had worked for the

Blame

British Antarctic Survey, and had personal experience of a leopard seal attack. A few years earlier, he had helped draft the standard operating procedures for diving in the Antarctic after a young researcher had been killed by a leopard seal at the nearby Rothera Research Station, so there was no better person for the job.

The day of the swim started off clear, but there was a storm building and the clouds looked ominous. Our team had two boats – one driven by Damon Stanwell-Smith, and one by our Norwegian expedition leader, Jørn Henriksen. Jørn and Professor Tim Noakes measured out the kilometre route, while Stanwell-Smith drove his boat up and down to check for leopard seals.

It was becoming dark by the time Damon gave us the all clear. While he monitored the area, Jørn drove me to the shoreline and put me out on a rocky outcrop, which is where I did my final preparation.

Once I start taking off my clothes, the transition from being warm and dry to getting in the water has to be quick and seamless so that I don't lose too much body heat. I had already inserted the thermometer that would measure my core body temperature. (I'll leave the exact placing of that one up to your imagination – suffice to say that it is probably my least favourite part of swim preparation!) As soon as I whipped off my top, Jonathan slipped the antennae into the socket on the back of my chest monitor. Then he guided me down to the water's edge, and gave me the RAF countdown just the way we'd practised it during our training at the I&J factory in Cape Town.

I would have preferred to swim a straight kilometre, but the Prof felt that it wouldn't be fair to swim in one direction only, in case there was a current. So I struck out for our halfway mark, an iceberg 500m away.

The water was crystal clear and a stunning turquoise blue – the only time I've seen anything like it is in the Maldives. But in the Indian Ocean, when you look down, you've got turtles and manta rays, coral and tropical fish. Here the water temperature was 0°C, I had an iceberg on the horizon and Adélie penguins darting back and forth beneath me. I tried not to think of them as the favourite food of leopard seals.

Conquering fear doesn't make you brave. But learning to work with it makes you better at what you do. The trick is to put your fear in its proper place. I was learning, through our experiments with anticipatory thermo-genesis, that I needed the fear to help me raise my core body temperature. So I tried to be grateful to the leopard seals. Still, I hoped they would keep their distance!

> *'Conquering fear doesn't make you brave. But learning to work with it makes you better at what you do. The trick is to put your fear in its proper place.'*

When I got to the halfway turn, it had started snowing, and I was starting to feel really cold. Then the snowstorm hit in earnest, and it started to come down in fat, heavy flakes. The Prof was on the boat under a blanket watching the monitor, while Jonathan Dugas wrote my vital statistics on a whiteboard to keep me informed.

And then the information just stopped coming.

(I didn't know it yet, but the pen had frozen.) Minutes passed. The whiteboard was sopping wet with snow. The pen wasn't working. Then it froze. Jonathan found another one, but it slipped from his frozen hands and fell into the bottom of the boat. He was bent double trying to find it, with the Prof on his knees helping him. No one was looking at me. 'What is happening?' I shouted. 'I need info!'

That information was crucial for me; knowing that my core temperature hadn't dropped below safe levels helped me mentally to withstand the effects of the severe cold. I needed to know how much time had elapsed, and how much distance was left, so that I could judge whether I needed to go faster to stave off the cold, or conserve my energy for the distance. But the information just wasn't coming.

I put my head out of the water and pleaded for some numbers. I used a few choice expletives that I would never use with someone like the Prof, but I was desperate! He jumped up, faced the storm and started bellowing: '300 metres to go ... 250 to go ... You can do this, Lewis! LET'S GO!!' In a second, the Prof had turned from doctor and scientist into coach. And he got me to the end of the kilometre.

The Zodiac pulled up as I climbed up onto the starting rock. The Prof high-fived me, put a big blanket around me and we sped as fast as we could back to the ship. I was still feeling fresh, and I was so excited – we had done it! Not only had we just completed the world's southernmost swim, but swimming conditions just didn't get tougher than the ones we'd faced.

It was only once I was back on board and in the hot shower, listening to the Prof read out my core body temperatures, that I realised nobody else was smiling. Worse, I could tell by their faces that there was something seriously wrong.

The Prof gave it to me straight. 'I'm sorry, Lewis,' he said. 'But in our rush to get you into the water, we forgot to put the watch on your wrist.'

That watch carries all the statistics from my heart monitor. Without that watch, the science part of the swim was incomplete. The team had flown halfway across the world and sailed across the infamous Drake Passage to help me do the

— Yak 6 —

> *'For the sake of that science, I would have to do it all over again. I wanted to scream.'*

swim safely and to get the information. For the sake of that science, I would have to do it all over again.

I wanted to scream. You don't want to do such a dangerous swim more than once. I wanted to crucify whoever was responsible. I just really wanted to blame somebody. But luckily I held my tongue. During our training, the watch had sometimes been put on by Lara Dugas (Jonathan's wife, a specialist in exercise nutrition), sometimes by Jonathan and sometimes by me. The point is that we hadn't designated the watch as someone's specific responsibility.

I went to the dining room, had a meal, and asked myself, 'Who is really to blame here?' Then I realised: *I am responsible*. The buck stops with me. I have to take 100% responsibility.

In the SAS, I learned about the importance of a blame-free culture. In the Regiment, you will get total indemnity for a mistake, as long as you put up your hand immediately and take responsibility.

Lives and situations depend on it. I contrasted that with my time in the legal profession, and the flurries of memos that would circulate around the office when people tried to duck responsibility. I always thought it was such a waste of time. Why not just try to solve the problem immediately?

Blame doesn't help. Not only is it completely pointless, but blame fired off in the heat of the moment can leave scars that last a lifetime. Blame can have a devastating effect on the morale of the team, and on the individuals within it.

'Blame can have a devastating effect on the morale of the team, and on the individuals within it.'

One of the things we learned from the Petermann Island swim was that we had been working without a basic checklist. Here we were at the cutting edge of sport and science, but we had neglected that fundamental basic! We drew up a checklist then and there.

We also planned the next swim. Our ship was turning around at Petermann Island, heading north again along the Antarctic Peninsula. So Jørn Henriksen and I went to the bridge and looked at the return route on a nautical chart. 'Right,' I asked him, 'where's the next best place to do a swim?'

Without hesitating, he put his finger down on Deception Island.

— Yak 7 —

Believe

....

The essence of any great achievement is to believe in your purpose.

....

There are few things as thrilling as seeing a whale surging out of the ocean and making a massive great splash as it hits the water again. When you are kayaking, and this huge leviathan comes up beneath you, it fills you with awe. And to think that we nearly lost the whole lot of them.

Thirty years ago, world whale populations were in a state of collapse, until the majority of nations agreed to stop commercial whaling. Since South Africa enacted laws prohibiting whaling in its coastal waters, it has seen a seven per cent increase in southern right whales year on year. It just shows what human beings can do when they have a common purpose.

Just how close we came to losing these magnificent creatures was brought powerfully home to me when I was attempting the longest swim ever undertaken in a polar region.

Deception Island, off the tip of the Antarctic Peninsula, is the most astonishing place. The horseshoe-shaped caldera provides one of the safest harbours in the region. It was created by a volcano that is still active today, so when you enter the bay from the open ocean, with icebergs everywhere, you find yourself surrounded by black beaches, snow-white peaks, and steam coming off the water. It's like a scene from a James Bond movie.

There used to be a whaling station there, until the volcano got the better of it; we were told that the water sometimes gets so hot that it melts the paint off ship's hulls. When we got there the water temperature ranged between 1°C and 3°C, which was still comfortably warmer than the swim I had done just two days earlier.

The Deception Island swim had not been planned; it came about because of what happened at Petermann Island, the original site for our attempt at the world's southernmost swim. Of course we had wanted to complete that swim successfully the first time, but when I finished the kilometre

I discovered that, in the rush to get into the sea, we'd forgotten to put on the watch that monitors my heartbeat – a crucial part of the data-collecting apparatus.

Perhaps this is a good time to explain some of the science behind my swims. People talk about the fact that I only wear a Speedo swimming costume when I swim in freezing water, but in fact, I also wear a lot of technology. I've got a watch on my wrist, and a monitor strapped around my chest, which has an antenna sticking out at the back. There is a cable running from this to an iPhone-sized receiver strapped to my backside. That receiver is connected to a plastic rectal thermometer, which measures my core temperature while I'm in the water.

> *'People talk about the fact that I only wear a Speedo swimming costume when I swim in freezing water, but in fact, I also wear a lot of technology.'*

All this equipment sends a signal to a laptop computer in the support Zodiac. From there, Professor Tim Noakes can tell how long I've been in the water, and monitor my heart rate and core body temperature. He plots this information on a graph, from which he extrapolates how long I am likely to live.

If that sounds dramatic, perhaps I need to explain that the danger time is not so much while I am in the water, but after I get out of it. That's because my core temperature will continue to go down for a while before it starts coming up again. We call this the 'afterdrop'. This is how it happens: as soon as I dive into the water, my veins and capillaries close down so that blood can be diverted from my extremities to my core, to try and keep it warm in order to protect my vital organs. When I get out and rush into a hot shower, the capillaries open up again to send that core blood to my extremities. But because those extremities are frozen, that blood is rapidly cooled and returns back into my heart, cooling it down. The Prof takes all of this into account when he makes the judgment call as to how long I can safely be in the water.

Knowing all this, you can imagine how we felt at the end of the Petermann Island swim. We had

Believe

spent so much time preparing and doing the scientific research, and now we didn't have the data we needed. Going back into the water was the last thing I felt like doing, but it was the first thing I had to do.

And so, two days later, we arrived at Deception Island. Because we knew the water was going to be warmer, we decided to try for a much longer swim. But when we tested the water about 100m from the shore it was still only 2°C. A bit further down the coast it was 1°C, and the warmest patch of water we found was 3°C. So instead of a four- or five-kilometre swim, we settled on 1.6km – still the longest swim in a polar region by far. We reckoned it would take me about 30 minutes – nearly twice as long as the Petermann Island swim, which had taken 18 minutes.

A family of Adélie penguins watched me prepare on the beach, next to a pile of discarded metal left over from the old whaling station. There were some big rusted cauldrons that I now realise must have once been used for melting whale blubber. But at the time, because I was concentrating on getting the equipment exactly right, I didn't put two and two together.

I started swimming from the shore. It was very shallow to begin with, so I had to run a bit before I was in water deep enough to surge away. The difference between 0°C and 2°C degrees is significant, and I felt really strong for the first 20 or 30 strokes. That is, until I looked down.

I just could not believe what I was seeing beneath me. There were whale bones everywhere. They literally covered the sea floor: jaw bones, rib bones, long white spines. I was swimming in a whale graveyard.

> *'I just could not believe what I was seeing beneath me. There were whale bones everywhere. They literally covered the sea floor.'*

The depth of the water varied, and at times it was so shallow that when I took a stroke my hands touched the bones. I thought of how they slaughtered those whales, and threw their remains and their skeletons back into the sea. I was so revolted by what I was seeing that I wanted to move the swim elsewhere. But the logistics of stopping, getting everyone into the boat, moving to another part of the bay and then reheating me to start the swim over would have been time-consuming. We'd come to Deception Island aboard an expedition tourist ship, and the captain had a schedule to keep. So I made myself push on. And the more I pushed on, the more bones I saw.

All through that swim, I thought of those peaceful giants of the world's oceans, how beautiful they are, and how we came so close to annihilating them for the sake of oil for our lamps, and to lubricate the machinery of our industrial age.

It took me just over 30 minutes to complete the mile, and it took me to the edge. The longest swim we had ever done in such extreme temperatures was 20 minutes. We didn't know how that extra time would affect me, but it wasn't looking good.

There was one piece of information the Prof still needed. As unpleasant as the rectal thermometer is to swim with, the one the Prof used to measure my muscle temperature was much worse; it has a sharpened end, which he simply rammed like a spear straight into my upper thigh! 'Just hold it there, Lewis,' he told me, as we raced back to the ship in our little Zodiac.

My core temperature was dropping rapidly, but I still had to make my way up the gangplank, and past a group of tourist well-wishers, with that huge thermometer rammed deep into my leg.

We must have looked like a strange caterpillar coming on board: I was wet and barefoot with a spear sticking out of my thigh; Jonathan Dugas was guiding me along the slippery, icy gangway, the Prof followed without taking his eyes off the open laptop, and Lara Dugas brought up the rear holding all the cables so that none of us would trip.

The Prof kept urging me to stay awake, but it was only once I was sitting under the hot shower that I registered the concern on his face. My core temperature was still dropping. As he read out the numbers – 36°C, 35.5°C, 35°C – I prayed that the drop would bottom out. I passed the point of clinical

'I passed the point of clinical hypothermia and still the numbers kept dropping.'

hypothermia and still the numbers kept dropping. I knew that at 32°C you start getting cardiac arrhythmias; at 29°C you will soon leave this world. I could feel my heart occasionally judder and I knew I should be panicking, but I just felt sleepy because my body was shutting down.

My temperature dropped for 30 minutes, even while I was in the hot shower. Finally, at 33°C, it bottomed out and slowly started rising again and I saw the relief on the Prof's face.

I knew this swim would provide valuable new data – nobody had swum in that kind of temperature before over that kind of distance. It was gratifying to be contributing to a ground-breaking study – and at the same time to complete both the most southerly swim and the longest polar swim ever undertaken. But as we sailed back to Ushuaia, in Argentina, I realised that something even greater had come out of this swim.

I knew now that I had to stand up and start speaking about protecting our environment. From that moment on, every swim should have the aim of inspiring people to protect and preserve the world's oceans and all that live in them.

There are many different kinds of self-belief. Some people seem to be born with it – look at great sportsmen like Pelé, Muhammad Ali or Usain Bolt. Other people's self-belief is nurtured from the outside, by caring parents or teachers, or because they were part of an elite team and stepped up to the level of excellence around them.

For others, self-belief is born from experience; they climb a mountain and the thrill of achievement makes them want to go higher. They do Kilimanjaro, then Mount McKinley, and then one day they stand at the bottom of Everest and they believe they can get to the top of it, because of the experience they've built up for themselves.

There is another kind of self-belief that can take your performance to another level altogether. The tragedy is that few people connect with it. It's the kind of belief that comes from the heart. The kind that says, 'I'm doing this because it's what I was meant to do with my life.'

The most powerful form of self-belief comes from believing in something greater than you.

Because when you've got purpose, everything becomes possible.

> *'When you've got purpose, everything becomes possible.'*

Think of Desmond Tutu and Nelson Mandela in South Africa. Think of Burmese leader Aung San Suu Kyi or Mother Teresa. Despite some of the most horrendous circumstances, they just kept going. Each of them believed utterly in their cause.

My cause is the ocean.

As a young boy growing up in Cape Town, the sea was a constant presence in my life. I don't recall seeing many whales as a child, but over the past 30 years I have come to rely on the fact that the southern rights will be there in winter and spring, breaching and tail slapping with their calves by their sides. How awful that we still call them by the name used by whalers to indicate the 'right' whale to kill.

That swim at Deception Island was both an ending and a beginning for me. Up to then, my swimming had mostly been about being the first. But my swims in the Arctic and in Antarctica had made me aware of the harm being done to our oceans and of the need to do something about it. It would take a while for these thoughts to take shape, but the idea of swimming with a purpose – rather than just to be first – was increasingly on my mind.

— Yak 8 —

Push

....

Sometimes you just have to push past 'no'.

....

Every harbourmaster thinks their harbour is the busiest in the world, and the Sydney harbourmaster is no exception.

In early 2006 I was preparing for a crucial swim. I only needed one more ocean to become the first person to complete the Holy Grail of swimming: a long-distance swim in every ocean of the world. I had already swum in the Atlantic, the Arctic, the Southern (Antarctic) and the Indian. Only the Pacific remained. A long-distance swim in all five oceans of the world would be analogous to the Seven Summits, which mountaineers do. But the difficulty with the Five Oceans is that there are only a handful of swimmers who could do a long-distance swim in the freezing waters of the Arctic and Antarctic.

We mulled over a few options for our Pacific

venue – Bora Bora, Los Angeles, Tokyo … Finally, we settled on Sydney in Australia.

Now, Sydney Harbour is a busy place, and I assumed I was gong to need permission to do the swim. So I paid a visit to the harbourmaster.

I introduced myself and told him about the epic journey I had just been though. I told him I wanted to do my final swim in Australia because Australians love swimming. They can relate to it, and they would understand what I'd been through. I told him that I would like to start the swim from outer Manly Beach, swim through the Sydney Heads, and finish at the most iconic building in the southern hemisphere, the Sydney Opera House. I said I planned to do it in the next couple of days when the weather was good, and that I just wanted to confirm that all was OK and find out who we should contact on the radio channels if we had any difficulties.

'Uh, let me just stop you there, mate,' the harbourmaster said. 'This is a very busy harbour. We have ferries, we have yachts, we have tugs, we have cruise ships, and we have container ships. Having you swimming along at a few kilometres per hour presents a real danger. One of the ships could steer away to avoid you and have a collision with another ship or run aground, or someone could get hurt because of this endeavour of yours.

'I don't want to be a spoilsport,' he went on, 'but we have had swims before in the Sydney Harbour and the organisers have had to secure two or three million dollars of insurance in the event that something goes wrong.' I told him I understood, thanked him politely, and walked out, thinking it was unlikely I'd be able to find an insurer to underwrite the swim.

I met Nick Peterson at the Sydney Opera House. We stood there looking at the scenery, and we didn't know what to do. Both of us are lawyers, both of us respect the law, but the more we went over it, the more we felt that the harbourmaster was being a little bit over-zealous.

For one thing, we were going to be swimming along the edge of the coastline to the Sydney Opera House. Admittedly, I'd have to cross the main shipping lane and a few ferry routes – but that could be done safely. Secondly, we were going to have a catamaran alongside us, with lookouts and a radio on board. If anything happened, I would be able to get onto the boat quickly.

We had a very experienced crew lined up, including Australian swimmer Ben McGuire, who would swim alongside me. I had safely swum across the English Channel, the busiest shipping lane in the world. And, we thought, there are so many pleasure yachts just cruising around Sydney Harbour; is this really a genuine risk?

I'm not a rule-breaker by nature. But there are times when you need to untangle yourself from red tape. Because the truth is, if you wait for permission some things will simply never happen.

'The truth is, if you wait for permission, some things will simply never happen.'

Nick and I looked at one another, and he said, 'You know, Lewis, by the time the authorities wake up in the morning, we'll already be in the harbour. We'll tell the press to meet us at the finish at 10am.'

The next morning felt just like an SAS operation. There we were, at 5am, and it was barely light. We had two other boats with us – the catamaran with Ben McGuire's dad and his girlfriend aboard, and Nick in a little Zodiac support boat.

The danger from shipping was one thing, but my bigger fear was sharks. Shark attacks occur every year in Australian waters, so Ben had brought his electronic anti-shark device, which Nick attached to the side of the Zodiac.

> *'The danger from shipping was one thing, but my bigger fear was sharks.'*

We dived under a few waves, and we were off. Breathing to our right, we swam past the beautiful cliffs of North Head, and it was just fantastic. Ben was swimming powerfully next to me, and my mate Nick was on the boat alongside us. But at the back of my mind was the nagging worry about the harbourmaster. I didn't want any of us to get arrested.

We made it through The Heads, where we

found that the current was extremely strong. We struggled to get through, and when we finally did I lifted my head up and said, 'Nick, we've made it!' Our journey, which had started many years previously, to complete a long-distance swim in every ocean of the world, was nearly over. Ahead of me, the Sydney Opera House glistened in the sunlight. And behind it was the Sydney Harbour Bridge. It was one of the most beautiful sights I had ever seen.

It was at that point that Nick, on the Zodiac, cleared his throat. 'Guys,' he said, 'we have a slight problem.' With a nervous little smile on his face he went on: 'As I was going through the waves, the anti-shark device ripped off the boat.'

'What do you mean it ripped off the boat?' I couldn't believe what I was hearing. The water around me felt suddenly that much more treacherous.

'Well,' Nick replied, 'I think I didn't really tie a very secure knot.' This from a man who'd rappelled out of helicopters many times in the SAS! In the meantime, I made sure I swam right next to

Ben for the rest of the distance. I'm not a betting man, but the odds just felt better that way.

We struck out once more, heading for the Sydney Opera House. Shortly afterwards, I heard a helicopter above us. My first thought was, 'The harbourmaster has bust us!' I looked up and saw someone hanging out of it with a video camera and realised it was a news team. I also realised that we had to move quickly, before the authorities got wind of us.

About a kilometre from the end of the swim we came up to the Royal Australian Navy base on Garden Island. The exclusion zone around the base would require us to swim another kilometre or so out of our way. I was so exhausted at this point that I just thought, bugger it, I'm going to swim through this exclusion zone. As I reached the middle of the zone, a diver in scuba gear came shooting straight up out of the depths in front of me. Again I thought, 'We're bust, it's an Australian Navy diver.' Then I saw the camera in his hand. 'Slow down mate, slow down!' It was another reporter determined to get his shot.

— Yak 8 —

Now I had media above me and below me, but when I heard the siren I knew, this time, it really WAS the harbourmaster. But Nick put his Zodiac between us and said to me, 'Just go for it, Lewis. I'll deal with this.'

> *'Nick put his Zodiac between us and said to me, "Just go for it, Lewis. I'll deal with this."'*

I put my head down, and Ben and I swam as fast as we could to the end. When my feet touched the shore, I felt such joy and elation at having successfully completed a swim in every ocean of the world. I looked back and saw that Nick was still arguing with the harbourmaster – he'd kept him occupied long enough for us to get to the little beach!

Here's the crucial point: I would not have made the swim at all if I'd allowed myself to get tangled up in red tape. If you want something badly enough, you just have to make it happen. It's all too easy for people to say 'no' to a request, especially when they are in a position of authority. But if you go ahead and start something, it's much more difficult for them to stop you. Better not to give them that option to begin with, and be prepared to say 'sorry' afterwards.

The next day the headline in the *Sydney Morning Herald* read: 'Pom causes waves in Sydney Harbour'. We wouldn't have wanted it any other way.

— Yak 9 —

Follow

Don't be limited by other people's expectations. If you know a better way to do something, follow your own set of rules.

Finland is a beautiful country, but it has some of the world's most bizarre annual events. These include the World Wife Carrying Championships, the Air Guitar World Championships, the World Mobile (phone) Throwing Championships ... and of course the World Winter Swimming Championships.

In early 2006 I received an email from the Finnish Winter Swimming Association. They had heard that I'd just done the swim in Antarctica and wanted to invite me to participate in the World Winter Swimming Championships in Oulu. I had never been to Finland before, and I thought it sounded fun, so I accepted the invitation.

At around the same time I got a phone call from an American producer of the HBO show *Real Sports with Bryant Gumbel*. They were interested in doing an investigative piece on anticipatory thermo-genesis, and wanted to know where they might film me doing a swim. So I said, 'Why not come along to Finland?'

I told them there would be lots of international swimmers there – from Scandinavia, the UK, Australia and Russia. It occurred to me that I had never raced a Russian before. So I said something I almost came to regret. 'A Brit against the Russians,' I told him. 'This is going to be the REAL Cold War!'

I was just trying to big-up the event a bit, and it worked. I could just about hear his ears pricking up all the way over the Atlantic. The spin had started.

The UK TV crews I had dealt with had always been small – usually a two-person cameraman-and-presenter team. The Americans do things differently. The HBO team arrived with three cameramen, a presenter, a director and a handful of other crew.

Follow

We arrived in minus 17°C to find men with long chainsaws cutting the top layer from the ice covering the Oulujoki River. After an enormous crane lifted out huge blocks of ice, the instant pool makers put in lane ropes, and began blasting warm water over the surface to keep the 25m pool from freezing over.

Later that day, I looked at the programme and suddenly discovered that the entire competition consisted of a series of 25m races, all of them breaststroke. I couldn't believe it. I hadn't come all the way up here to take a cold bath!

'Surely you've got some other events?' I asked the organiser, Mariia Yrjö-Koskinen. But that was it. I told her I wanted to swim crawl, and a lot more of it. 'In Finland we are very experienced in cold-water swimming,' she told me. 'Our doctors tell us that if you dive in and swim with your head in the water it can be such a shock to your body that you could even have a heart attack.' At this point I knew very well that I could do a kilometre – I had just done it in Antarctica. 'Mariia,' I said, 'we've got to have a serious race.' She looked doubtful. 'I don't know anyone who is prepared to swim crawl,' she said, 'or who is prepared to do more than 25 metres.'

What was I going to do? Not only did I have the HBO crew with me, but Trans World Sport and the BBC had also arrived to do features on me. This was going to be very embarrassing. So I went off to find me some Russians.

The Russian swimmers were headed up by Colonel Vladimir Lutov, a distinguished grey-haired officer and a cold-water swimmer of some reputation. Through a translator, I introduced myself and told him that 25m was no challenge at all. 'Would you be prepared to race me over two kilometres?' (I was hoping we could settle on one kilometre, but I was allowing for a bit of horse-trading.)

Lutov looked at me long and hard. 'Me think about it,' he said, and walked away.

The competitors had all gathered at the hotel to sample Finnish vodka. Besides the Russians and the Finns, there were some Swedes, some Germans, a gang of Brits, half a dozen Australians and some

Follow

Irish. The Australians were backpacking through Europe and thought this sounded like a good idea! I made friends with Alistair Petrie and Lucy Scott, two actors from London and members of the Tooting Bec Swimming Club, who got right on board with my Russian challenge.

The next day we watched the 25m breaststroke heats. The competitors would use a wooden ladder to climb down into the freezing water. They would hold on to the ladder until the starting gun went off, and then swim as fast as they could to the other side. Then they would jump out, high-five each other and head straight into a sauna. We watched heat after heat after heat of this. Then the first day of the two-day event was over. It was time to pin down Colonel Lutov.

'Me not race you,' he told me when I found him. 'Two other comrades will race you. One on either side.' How far? 'Five hundred metres.'

My mind went into overdrive. Just what was his strategy? Why did he want me to swim against two men? Why me in the middle? Would one cut in ahead of me and slow me down so the other one could race ahead and beat me? I started seeing Russians on every corner, and they all seemed to be eyeballing me. The week before, I had written a press release: 'British swimmer challenges the Russians!' and sent it out to Reuters, AFP and the ITAR-TASS press agency in Moscow. Had I insulted these people in my haste to get a story going? When a bus full of Russian journalists arrived, it only added to the media circus.

I was starting to wish I hadn't started all this Cold War nonsense. Alistair and Lucy didn't help either. 'The pride of Great Britain is resting on you, Lewis!' they told me that evening. Maybe it was the Finnish vodka talking, but I was beginning to feel rather unsettled.

At the dinner table that evening, the Russians stared at me throughout the meal. Later on, they seemed to line the corridor to my room – and it didn't feel like a guard of honour. If these were intimidation tactics, they were working. I became so paranoid that I considered moving the wardrobe in front of my door. Or sleeping in the hotel lounge, where there would be witnesses!

When I woke up the next morning, I wasn't thinking of Russian shenanigans. I was thinking of the Fosbury Flop, the move that revolutionised the high jump at the 1968 Summer Olympics. Before Dick Fosbury came along and turned the world of high-jumping upside down (quite literally), everyone was doing the scissor jump. But after Fosbury won his gold medal, everybody started to curl backwards over the high jump. Similarly here, every previous race in the World Winter Swimming Championships had been done over 25m, and nobody had ever dared put their head in the icy water. Everyone was waiting to see what would happen in today's race.

My Russian rivals were Alexander Brylin and Vladimir Nefatov. Brylin is a massive barrel-chested man from the Russian east coast, near the Chinese border. He arrived poolside wearing wetsuit shorts, which he'd pulled right up to his chest to keep himself as warm as possible. He was flanked by a bevy of gorgeous Russian girls, and looked like Rocky Balboa coming out for a fight.

Vladimir was dressed the same way, but at this point I would look like a nit-picker if I told them the challenge was to wear just a Speedo swimming costume, cap and goggles. But when the rules were declared I made it clear that we could swim whatever stroke we wanted.

Getting undressed in minus 17°C is brutal. The water in the pool was 0.5°C – just above freezing – but knowing there was a burly Russian on either side of me took the edge off the cold. 'Take your marks, get set ...'

> *'Getting undressed in minus 17°C is brutal. The water was 0.5°C – just above freezing – but knowing there was a burly Russian on either side of me took the edge off the cold.'*

And then we were off. I gave it everything I had from the start, swimming the fastest crawl that I could. I was breathing on the right-hand side, and I could see the Brits shouting and waving their little national flags. Then I saw the Russian supporters next to them flying massive Russian flags. That made me swim even harder.

The ice was too sharp to do a tumble turn at the end of the lane, but when I started back I saw the two Russians steaming towards me with the fastest breaststroke I'd ever witnessed in my life. I still didn't know what their strategy was, and I was worried that they might be holding something back, so I kept up my pace. At 50m I had opened the gap, at 200m I could see I was really taking good distance out of these guys. Why weren't they doing crawl?

When I slapped my hand down on the ice at the end of 500 metres, I turned around and saw that I had beaten Alexander by 100m, and Vladimir by 150m.

Now there was a problem I hadn't thought of: swimming etiquette holds that you don't get out of the pool until everyone is finished the race, so I had to stay there in this freezing cold water and wait for them. I jumped out just before Alexander came streaming in. All his girls gathered around, screaming, but he ignored them when he climbed out of the water. Instead he came straight over to me and gave me an enormous great bear hug. Vladimir joined us a few minutes later. I handed Alexander my swimming cap, with its Union flag, he handed me his one emblazoned with the Russian flag.

Suddenly, all the bravado was finished.

There's something very special about swimming, something that happens when you strip down to the bare essentials and endure that kind of challenge. Alexander and I couldn't even speak without a translator, but from that moment we became close friends.

In our different ways, we'd each been prepared to challenge the status quo. We knew that it was possible to swim the 500m, and we wanted to take everyone else into the realm of this possibility.

'We knew that it was possible to swim the 500m, and we wanted to take everyone else into the realm of this possibility.'

You often see people

doing something a certain way, because the conventional wisdom says it has to be so. Before our swim, 'conventional wisdom' said that if you dived into freezing water you could have a heart attack and die on the spot. But nobody had tested this assumption. So we challenged it – and we changed the sport of cold-water swimming forever.

The organisers decided to do the next World Winter Swimming Championships in London. The water wasn't quite as cold, but a long-distance head-down crawl race was an undisputed part of the programme. And many swimmers did it.

Don't ever be afraid to follow your own path. Sometimes when you change the rules, you discover a much better way of doing things.

— Yak 10 —

Grind

Sometimes the hard way is not just the best way, it's the only way.

In the middle of winter, Norway's Nigards Glacier looks just like any of the icy mountain valleys around it. But in the summer, when the snow starts to melt, it reveals its true beauty. The glacier is a light turquoise blue; it always looks to me like a blue tongue licking into the lake beneath it.

It's an extraordinarily lovely sight. But of all the extraordinary things I've seen in my life, my most memorable is the General in a little red rowboat at the foot of this glacier. The sight was not memorable because of the scenery, but because the General was performing an act of grindingly hard work that bordered on the heroic.

The boat wasn't moving much; it was completely iced in. But the General stood at the bow, hacking away at chunks of ice in front of the boat.

With him were Jonathan Dugas and a Norwegian glacier guide, swinging their own ice picks in unison.

Now, here's what you need to know about the General. He is tall – over two metres – and striking, in the sense that, as soon as he starts speaking, people are drawn to him. He has a unique ability to feel as comfortable dining with royalty as he is having a sandwich with a Nepalese Sherpa on a Himalayan mountain. He loves to encourage people, and his enthusiasm is always infectious.

I met General Tim Toyne Sewell when he was the head of Goodenough College, the postgraduate hall of residence for overseas students, where I stayed when I first came to London. There were over 600 postgraduate students from all over the world at that residence, which meant that the General had more than 600 fans. Everybody adored him. And the feeling was quite mutual. The General loved being around young people. As former Commandant of the Royal Military Academy Sandhurst, the General had been in charge of training new officers in the British Army. He took up the position at Goodenough on his retirement.

I asked him to come to Norway in 2006 to oversee safety while I attempted the world's longest swim in ice water. It was the first time I experienced him in the field, as it were. He would go on to accompany me on my Thames swim, in the Maldives and up Everest, and I think this story illustrates why.

We chose the Nigards Glacier Lake as the perfect site for the swim because we could get to this part of Norway relatively quickly from London (via Bergen). As soon as we got word that the lake was beginning to thaw, which is the moment you can be sure that the water is just above 0°C, we could get there within a day.

Once the ice starts to melt, it happens quickly. Our man on the ground was Peder Kjærvik, who runs the Nigards Glacier Museum. If anyone knows that glacier, it's Peder. I phoned Peder on a daily basis to check the status of the ice, and finally he told us it was ready.

But when we arrived at the lake, we discovered

> *'But when we arrived at the lake, we discovered that it was still frozen all the way to the glacier edge.'*

that it was still frozen all the way to the glacier edge. To be fair to Peder, there was a little sliver of water right in front of the glacier, where the fresh water runs off the mountain and into the lake. It was enough to swim in, but its location presented us with a logistical nightmare.

The problem was that the car park was way over on the other side of the ice. How were we going to get me, after I'd just swum 1,250m in icy water, over this slippery, frozen expanse to a place where I could warm up? I would definitely be hypothermic, and there would be no time to mess around.

I sat down with my team – the General, Jonathan Dugas and Martin Jenkins – to go over our options. My first thought was to build a huge bonfire on the edge of the lake; as soon as I finished the swim, I could go straight there to defrost. We'd done that successfully after my swim at the North Cape. But the General pointed out that we were in a part of the world that gets on average 235 days of rain a year; the chances were excellent that a heavy downpour would put a fire out. We contemplated walking the rocky pathway along the edge of the lake, but it was dangerously slippery and it would take me at least half an hour to get to the car park that way. That was simply too much time. 'If anything goes wrong, I want Lewis back and close to a road,' the General said.

That's when he had his eureka moment. 'We'll cut a pathway through the ice,' he said, 'from the face of the glacier all the way to the car park. And then we'll drive a boat in to come and collect you.'

Now, ice is a hard substance; when it flows down the mountain as a glacier it gouges out valleys. The ice on the lake was thick; getting through it would not be like digging powdery snow off the path to your front door. And the distance the General was contemplating was nearly a kilometre. 'He can't be serious!' I said out of earshot. But he was.

'Stand aside, Pugh,' he said. 'Stand aside.'

> *"Stand aside, Pugh," he said. "Stand aside." He looked over to a nearby group of Norwegian glacier guides. "Just give me some Norwegians and some ice picks!"'*

He looked over to a nearby group of Norwegian glacier guides. 'Just give me some Norwegians and some ice picks!'

Knowing the General's powers of persuasion, it didn't really surprise me that a number of glacier guides, as well as Jonathan and Martin, heeded his call for help. Next, the General commandeered the little red boat. And that's how I came to be watching a 65-year-old man cut a kilometre-long channel through ice as thick as his forearm was long. All for one of his former students who wanted to do a swim.

Of course I offered to help. But the General wouldn't hear of it. 'I need you fresh for this swim, Lewis,' he said, and sent me to sit beside the lake.

It took the General six hours to cut his way to the water in front of the glacier, during which time, amazingly, neither he nor any of his helpers caught an ice pick in the head! He rowed that boat all the way back to the car park, proud as punch that he'd got the job done. I was concerned about what would happen overnight, though, when the ice could refreeze. 'Lewis,' he said to me, 'I take each day as it comes. I'll worry about that in the morning.'

Sure enough, when the General woke at 5am, he discovered that the lake had frozen over during the night. We were scheduled to complete our swim in time for a live TV spot on BBC Breakfast at ten past eight. So there he was, back on the ice, going double speed to clear the channel. It took him two hours to clear the ice again, but he did it.

By the time I arrived at the lakeshore with the media in tow, the General had the crowd going. The local support had been amazing all through our preparation, but I had not expected such a show from the people of Jostedal, the narrow valley below the Nigards Glacier. The local schoolchildren were all there, waving Norwegian and British flags. They had made banners and posters saying: 'Go Lewis Pugh' and 'Heia! Heia! (Go, Go) from Jostedal'. There was even a five-man accordion band, in matching Nordic knit sweaters, on the shore entertaining the crowd. All of them had watched the General clear his channel. Now I had to step up to the task.

The water was unbelievably cold. And because we had such a narrow sliver to work with, I had to do six widths across to make the 1,250m I needed to set the world record. When I climbed out, I was well and truly frozen, but the little red boat sped me down 'the General's Channel' to the car, and from there I was raced to a hot shower, in all of five minutes.

Driving us back to Bergen the next day, I looked at the General's hands and saw that they were covered in bleeding blisters. But do you think he complained?

'Sometimes, Lewis,' he said to me, 'there is just no easy way to get the job done.'

'"Sometimes, Lewis," he said to me, "there is just no easy way to get the job done."'

We tend to look for the easiest way to do things, but achievements mean much more when you pay for them with hard work. And I will never forget the effort that one very special man and his team put in to help me to achieve my dream.

— Yak 11 —

Test

The most perfect of plans can fall apart when we forget to test our assumptions.

In all my wildest dreams – and some of them have gone to the very edges of the map – I never imagined that a swim down a river would be the one to seal my purpose.

When I completed my Sydney swim in 2006, many people believed I had attained the Holy Grail of swimming: a long-distance swim in all five oceans of the world. I knew it was a great achievement, but even so, at the end of it I couldn't help wondering, was it all just a box-ticking exercise?

As always, I turned to the General for advice. What next? 'You are doing all these swims around the world, Lewis,' he said, 'but you've never done a swim at home in Britain.' So I thought, why not the Thames? The river, which flows through Oxford, Windsor, London and Greenwich, is one of the best-known rivers in the world. Yet no one had ever swum its full length – 350km from source to sea.

The swim also presented an opportunity to promote a charitable cause. 'Find something close to your heart,' the General advised. A short while later I was walking in the Yorkshire Dales with my friend James Mayhew and his girlfriend Clare Kerr, who was an ambassador for the World Wide Fund for Nature (WWF). 'You are so passionate about the Arctic and Antarctica, and you've been telling us about all the changes you've been seeing,' she told me. 'Why don't you become a voice for those places?' I told her I wasn't an expert on climate change. 'You don't need to be,' she said. 'Don't try to be a scientist. Just tell people what you are seeing and share your passion. Ask people to help protect our environment – you could do it with WWF.'

Her words stopped me in my tracks. I'm one

> *"You are so passionate about the Arctic and Antarctica, and all the changes you've been seeing," she told me. "Why don't you become a voice for those places?"'*

Test

of those people who like to sit on an idea and let it percolate. I'm a great believer in the 4am test. Set your alarm clock to 4am. If the idea still feels good at that unearthly hour of the morning, you can trust it. I didn't need to sleep on this one. I knew it was a superb idea.

England was in the middle of the worst drought in living memory, and there were water restrictions throughout the south. 'We are going to have droughts and floods and they are going to become more extreme,' a WWF representative told me. 'Your swimming across the entire width of this country, when we have so little water, will really bring home that message.'

I called my friend Nic Marshall to join me on the recce. We started at the source of the Thames, just outside the village of Kemble in the Cotswolds, and followed the river all the way to London. It was late spring, and we drove along country roads, with cows grazing in the green fields, and the beautiful river winding its way under trees. We stopped at various bridges along the way to drop sticks into the river and time their speed; we worked out that the river was flowing at about 4km per hour. Since I can swim comfortably at 3km an hour, we estimated that it would take me about ten days to swim the entire length of the river. And then I didn't think about it again. That was my big mistake. It seemed a perfectly reasonable assumption. But it wasn't.

Two months later, when we arrived at the starting point for the swim, there was no water there. It was a blisteringly hot day. We consulted the Ordnance Survey map and realised that the river had dried up in the drought; there was no water anywhere for the first 40km. 'What are you waiting for, Lewis?' said the General. 'Start running!'

'There was no water anywhere. "What are you waiting for, Lewis?" said the General. "Start running!"'

I put on running shorts and a vest and started down the pathway along the river's edge with James Mayhew. I ran for 40km, in 39°C heat, before I came to anything deep enough to swim in. You can imagine how I had been looking forward to diving in and

Test

cooling off, but when I finally got into the water it was not at all refreshing; it was warm sludge. The Thames had become a stagnant pond.

I hoped the flow would improve as we went along, when other streams joined the river. But the next day there was no flow at all. And still no flow the day after that. This was going to be a problem.

I had been so busy during the preparation for the swim that I had only managed three training sessions a week, of between 40 and 50 minutes each. Not enough to prepare me to swim 350km with no flow whatsoever.

By the time we got to Oxford, the stagnant water had taken its toll and my stomach was absolutely rotten. I was so sick that the General took me to the local hospital and I spent the night in Emergency. The next day, he fetched me and

'I had been so busy during the preparation for the swim that I had only managed three training sessions a week, of between 40 and 50 minutes each. Not enough to prepare me to swim 350km with no flow whatsoever.'

took me back to the *Thames Crusader* (the narrow riverboat that was our home for the duration of the swim). But I wasn't allowed to rest on board. 'Every day is a swimming day, Lewis,' he said. I was so exhausted I could hardly walk, but I knew that every stroke was a stroke closer to the North Sea. So I got into the river and swam about 400m, which was all I could manage.

By this time we were well behind schedule, which presented a different kind of problem. We had estimated a 10-day swim. We had hired the support boat for 10 days. And my crew had put aside 10 days, some of them taking leave from their jobs, to be there with me for the duration. They had to pull strings and juggle commitments to continue supporting me. And they did.

The public support was equally amazing. Every day, people lined the banks of the river, following us along the towpaths, cheering us on. The press was all over us, too; it was August, and there wasn't much else to write about, so I filled up space in the newspapers. They even nicknamed me 'The People's Porpoise' after a porpoise that had swum up

Test

the river the year before. It had died, but I appreciated the sentiment.

Perhaps the most memorable moment of the journey was my first sight of Windsor Castle. We had covered 200km and, with the water so low, all I had seen until then was an endless muddy riverbank. Then I came around a bend in the river and saw the castle in all its majesty, while the river was suddenly covered with 20 or 30 beautiful white swans, which surged out from the banks as if anxious to repel this strange watery invader.

At this stage, the river was still warm and muddy and dark and filthy – besides the repeated stomach upsets I had a recurrent ear infection. But I also had Nic Marshall swimming with me every single day, James Mayhew paddling alongside me, the General and all the others who lent support at every turn, urging us on to the next bend whenever we thought we couldn't go any further.

I couldn't wait to get to Teddington, where the tidal Thames starts, so I could swim with the tide and let it pull me out to sea. But there was one more obstacle to overcome. And it was a serious one.

Teddington is also the official start of the Port of London, and the harbourmaster had threatened to arrest us if we attempted to swim through it. In his view, we were a serious danger to shipping. And to ourselves. 'This section of the river is too dangerous to swim in, there are currents which will suck you under.' Given where I had swum before, I didn't think this was his strongest argument. But he would not budge. After two lengthy meetings with the man, we knew that this was no idle threat. 'Why don't you just get out at Teddington and run to the North Sea?' the General said. But at this stage, having been through so much, there was no way I was going to let this jobsworth get in my way. There was no way I was going to let down all the people who had stuck with me. There was no way I was not

'At this stage, having been through so much, there was no way I was going to let this jobsworth get in my way. There was no way I was going to let down all the people who had stuck with me. There was no way I was not going to swim the entire length of that river!'

going to swim the entire length of that river – from source to sea!

Then our PR coordinator called with some game-changing news. There had been so much press coverage about the swim and our message that the Prime Minister wanted to meet us when we arrived at Westminster Bridge and discuss what Britain could do to tackle climate change. 'There are going to be hundreds of journalists as you emerge from the river in front of Parliament,' she said.

I called the harbourmaster right away. It didn't take long to convince him that arresting me there would look rather silly. 'Send one of your people round,' he said angrily, 'and we'll discuss how you are going to get down this river without any more fuss!' And then he slammed down the phone.

With a Port Authority tugboat shadowing us through the city, we got through Teddington and caught the outgoing tide. Finally, we were flying down that river! You know that you're in one of the most historic rivers on earth when you swim under the Chelsea Bridge and round the bend to see the Houses of Parliament in front of you, from river-eye level. Later I would pass St Paul's Cathedral, the great Tower of London and under Tower Bridge. But first, I made a stop for my meeting with the Prime Minister. Big Ben chimed 11 as I climbed out of the water.

I met Tony Blair at Downing Street and implored him to take meaningful action around climate change, not only to counter the impact it has on Britain, but also for developing countries, which haven't got the resources to properly mitigate against climate change. We have a moral duty to do everything we can in Britain to stop climate change, I told him.

Just past Greenwich, we reached the Thames Barrier, whose enormous rotating gates are designed to protect London from being inundated by high tides and storm surges. Swimming through the barrier was a reminder how vulnerable our cities are to the sea. On 31 January 1953, a combination of high winds and a very high spring tide caused a storm surge over 5.6m above normal in the North Sea. Coastal parts of eastern England were flooded, and 307 people lost their lives, while in the Netherlands more than 1,800 people died in the flooding.

We still had 70km to go to reach Southend-on-Sea, and our last stage would be a night swim. I jumped into the water in the early evening and the pain was instantaneous; I was in the middle of a huge patch of jellyfish and I was being stung all over. Nic Marshall jumped in immediately after me.

> *'I jumped into the water in the early evening and the pain was instantaneous; I was in the middle of a huge patch of jellyfish and I was being stung all over.'*

'Swim behind me,' he said. 'You need to finish this swim and be in a reasonable shape at the end to do interviews.' He wouldn't hear any argument, and for 70km he swam in front of me, pushing away those jellyfish. Finally, as the sun rose, the jellyfish disappeared and on the horizon we could see the beautiful pier of Southend-on-Sea. Nic had the most ghastly jellyfish stings all over his face and arms, but he swam with me to the very end.

It had taken us 21 days to reach the sea. I had

the kindest friends and the finest team anyone could ask for. We were all physically wrecked, but I had learnt a valuable lesson: always ask yourself what assumptions you are making, and whether those assumptions are valid. Do it continually, throughout the planning. My assumption that the river would be flowing nearly unhinged the whole expedition.

I took something else away from that swim: swimming is an incredible way to tell a story. It conveys a message very graphically – perhaps it has something to do with the fact there is very little separating a swimmer from the element he is in.

Shortly afterwards, the Prime Minister introduced a Bill in Parliament aimed at reducing the UK's production of greenhouse gases and at facilitating the transition to a low-carbon economy. In November 2008, the Bill passed into law as the Climate Change Act 2008.

— Yak 12 —

Open

Be open to possibilities and don't let yourself be limited by negative beliefs.

Of all the oceans, the Indian Ocean is the kindest and the most benevolent. The water is just so ... pleasant. Swimming there feels absolutely gorgeous.

So imagine my delight at swimming in the Indian Ocean, right on the equator. Swimming between dozens of little islands, each one more exquisite than the next. Beautiful golden beaches and palm trees, and the water between the islands every shade of blue. You dive into the ocean and look down on coral reefs with rainbow-coloured tropical fish and manta rays and turtles. It's paradise.

Except that this paradise is under grave threat. These are the lowest-lying islands in the world, and the spectre of rising sea levels means that the entire archipelago could one day disappear under water.

The island chain is the Maldives, a cigar-shaped archipelago 1,000km long and 140km wide. Most of the islands are less than half a metre in height – so low that when you swim just one kilometre off the coast you can barely see them.

And here's the hard inequity of it: the people of the Maldives have done virtually nothing to cause climate change, but they face the consequences of it daily. The President of the Maldives has been in negotiations with the Prime Minister of Sri Lanka to purchase a piece of his country so that, if and when his country submerges, he will have a place to take his people. He's a modern-day Noah.

I felt that this injustice needed to be highlighted. So I decided to gather a team and swim from island to island across the entire archipelago to give a face to the climate change that threatens the people of the Maldives.

The first person I called was the General. He didn't need much persuading to agree to come to the Maldives. The rest of the team were just as keen. And the Maldives Tourism Board kindly agreed to provide us with a boat.

Open

Now, given that the Maldives is a prime honeymoon destination, you would think that its tourism board would be well resourced. But that just isn't the case; behind the glossy image, the Maldives is a poor country. The tourism board did their best to help us, although, to be honest, when we first laid eyes on the big wooden boat they provided, we wondered whether it would make the journey. But we stowed our misgivings in the hold, along with our gear, and we set off.

The days were blissful. Each morning when we woke up, the General would say, 'Right, Lewis, off we go. Dive in and let's swim to the next island.' Then he would take off his shirt, rub sunblock on his head and shoulders and sit at the front of the boat and encourage me on. I remember swimming one day along the edge of a coral reef that plunged hundreds of metres into the darkness. Directly below me, an enormous manta ray came gliding along the edge of the reef, flapping its pectoral fins like wings. And then I looked up to see the General smiling down at me and looking so contented. And I thought, 'I have never swum in such a pleasant environment in my life.' I was swimming with the help of someone I respect deeply. And I was swimming with my heart, swimming to make a difference. The whole thing just felt right.

> *'I was swimming with my heart, swimming to make a difference. The whole thing just felt right.'*

Until the boat broke.

It was early afternoon, and we had just reached a big channel between two atolls. We were hoping to take advantage of the prevailing winds, which rose up every afternoon, to blow me along. 'Come on, Lewis,' the General said, eyeing the deep-blue channel. 'Let's just knock this one off.'

But less than half an hour into the crossing he motioned for me to stop. The boat's rudder had broken. The skipper put on an aqualung and jumped overboard. When he hadn't come up half an hour later, I realised we had serious problems. Another half-hour passed, and the General decided to give the skipper some moral support. So he donned a snorkel and mask and spent the next half hour div-

Open

ing down and coming back up again for air. When they both emerged from the water some time later, their faces conveyed the bad news: the boat wasn't fixable. We would have to get a replacement from the capital, Malé, and start this section of the swim again.

That's when the grim reality hit home. We had allowed ourselves ten days to complete the Maldives crossing, and we had three days left. There simply wasn't enough time to return to the capital, charter another boat, and resume the swim from this point. We couldn't extend our time either, since some team members had to be back at work on Monday morning. If we didn't finish the entire swim, we simply wouldn't get the kind of publicity we wanted for the cause. It was a bitter disappointment, and I felt thoroughly downhearted.

We also had a more immediate problem. The Indian Ocean runs like clockwork; in the early afternoon, the wind rises. We had expected this, but, without a rudder to steer us, the wind we had counted on to aid my swim was now blowing the boat towards a dangerous coral reef. The water was also too deep for us to throw out an anchor. We still had a bit of time, but we needed to do something.

Just then, I looked to the horizon and saw an enormous yacht. It was one of the most impressive luxury cruisers I had ever seen. (It had not one, but *two*, helicopter pads on deck!) I'd heard that Russian business tycoon Roman Abramovich had a yacht in the area, so I said to the General, 'Do you think that's Roman Abramovich's yacht? Imagine if it is, and he sails past and says, "Lads, let me take care of this."' I was just being flippant, but dreams are for free.

The General said, 'Give me your mobile phone.' He was commanding, but he had a huge smile on his face. I handed him my phone and listened to a most extraordinary conversation.

The General called Victoria Cork, Marketing Manager of Investec, our sponsors, in London. 'It's Timothy here,' he told her. 'And I'm in a spot of trouble.'

He gave Victoria the coordinates of our position. 'Could you please call the manager of Chel-

Open

sea Football Club, quick as you can?' he asked her. 'And could you get him to call Roman Abramovich and ask him if that's his yacht out there? And if it is, could he get them to pull around and come and rescue us?'

Now, I was holding myself back from laughing during all this. I mean, what were the chances? Call José Mourinho and ask him to call Roman Abramovich! Whatever next? But 30 minutes later, to my astonishment the phone rang. It was the yacht's skipper. 'I've just been instructed to hand you one of our tenders to finish the swim. Gentlemen, where would you like to go?'

We had a magnificent final three days in the Maldives. We finished the swim, and it received good coverage. Everybody was delighted, except one person – me. I was disappointed. Why? For the last 50km of that swim I kept asking myself, why didn't I call Roman Abramovich? Why hadn't I really believed he would come and help us? Why did I not think it was possible? Where had my limiting belief come from?

When we limit our beliefs about what is pos-

> *'When we limit our beliefs about what is possible, we don't ask for help. We're not even out of the stable and we've already given up the race.'*

sible, we don't ask for help. We're not even out of the stable and we've already given up the race. It's like wanting to play the game, but being too timid to get onto the pitch. That self-defeating, 'why bother' kind of thinking is particularly prevalent when it comes to making a difference in the world. Frankly, I should have known better.

Sailing back to Malé to fly home, I asked the General, 'Did you honestly believe that Abramovich would help us?'

'I'm a lot older than you are Lewis,' the General said to me, 'and this may sound silly. But I've gone throughout my life believing that everybody wants to help me.'

How empowering is that belief? A mind stretched to a new idea never returns to its original state. The General's words stretched me in that way. I would never be the same.

Working for a cause I care for gives me the

courage and the audacity to ask for help when circumstances seem improbable. The worst that can happen is that somebody can say 'no'. But they usually don't. The beautiful thing about human nature is that people really *do* want to help. We spend so much time worrying that people will say 'no'. Whereas, more often than not, they say 'yes'.

> *'We spend so much time worrying that people will say "no". Whereas, more often than not, they say "yes".'*

And, of course, I'm now a lifelong Chelsea supporter.

— Yak 13 —

Hope

You can do just about anything if you have hope. Lose it, and you don't stand a chance.

Planning an expedition is always something of a chicken-and-egg scenario. Which comes first? You've got to commit to doing the expedition, otherwise nobody is going to sponsor you. But without the sponsorship, you can't really get going. So you've actually got to commit before you've got the funds to carry it through.

When I started planning the North Pole swim, I wasn't very well known. I'd done the swims in Antarctica in 2005 and swum down the Thames in 2006, so people were beginning to hear about me, but I certainly wasn't a household name in 2007.

It's a very different scenario raising sponsorship for a big team or a household name. A Major League Baseball team will have a sponsorship agent who will go around to half a dozen different companies and present the package. Most importantly, the agent will be able to tell a potential sponsor what value they are going to get. If you sponsor the New York Yankees, you know your company is going to get a certain amount of guaranteed coverage on the TV news and sports channels every year.

That's just not the case when it comes to sponsoring an expedition. Here I was, just beginning to become known, and I was going to attempt the first swim across the North Pole. There aren't that many companies jumping to sponsor something like that. It's high risk, high reward. Agreed, there are very few firsts left in the world. And if I made it, it would be outstanding. But if I didn't, it could be really bad publicity – especially if I died in the process. And even if the expedition worked out, there was no guarantee that it wouldn't be eclipsed on the BBC or CNN by another big news story that day.

But I just had to keep hoping. When you have hope in the

'When you have hope in the future, you have power in the present. And when you lose that hope, your dream goes with it.'

Hope

future, you have power in the present. And when you lose that hope, your dream goes with it.

I don't just have a dream and expect it to turn out. Hope is not a strategy. I also have to put effort into it. Lots of effort. I write thousands of emails. I make hundreds of phone calls. I never stop fighting, until the very last minute. It's in my family's DNA.

I come from farming stock in South Africa on my grandmother's side. Some years are good years, some are average years, and some years are very tough, because the Eastern Cape is prone to terrible droughts. But what do they do when times are tough? They still plant seed.

A lot of people spend a lot of time hoping, without putting seed in the ground. Hope is the most important thing, but it can't stand on its own. You've got to be planting. You've got to take action.

'Hope is the most important thing, but it can't stand on its own. You've got to be planting. You've got to take action.'

The first person I called on to raise funds for

the North Pole swim was Hendrik du Toit from Investec. It didn't take much to persuade Hendrik that this was a good idea. He had seen me swim down the Thames, had seen the difficulties we had faced and overcome. Hendrik is a businessman, he has a pioneering spirit and is a very keen athlete. He loves running long distances, and he knew Professor Tim Noakes and the General well. So he was confident that the swim would be done safely, and would get huge media coverage. When we signed the deal I remember him saying: 'I want Investec to be the first to the North Pole!'

My next stop was Switzerland. I flew off to meet Jørgen Amundsen, the great-grandnephew of the explorer Roald Amundsen, the first person ever to reach the South Pole. Jørgen's whole family is about polar endeavour – he himself had walked the last few degrees to the North Pole. So it didn't feel so crazy to walk into Jørgen's office and tell him I wanted to swim across the North Pole.

Jørgen was the creative designer of a high-end watch company called Villemont. They wanted to bring out a new watch to compete with the big brands. To have someone swim across the North Pole with their watch – now that would be worth something. Not only was he in, he also wanted to come along on the trip.

Jørgen was an excellent skier, with polar experience. He was also fun to be around. I had done much of my training in Norway, and I love Norwegian people. So all the boxes were ticked.

We needed £180,000 to fund the expedition. I still hadn't got all the money, but this is how we stood: Investec had given us £120,000, and Villemont had given us £25,000. After travelling everywhere to organise the expedition and do the cold-water training with my team, I had £10,000 left in my savings. I put it all down. We still needed £25,000 to make the expedition happen.

We were a month away from setting sail. And £25,000 is not an insignificant amount of money. And here's another problem with swimming: the only branding space I have on my body is my backside and my head! And my backside is in the water most of the time. There's no value on my tracksuit because I won't be wearing that in the water.

— Yak 13 —

So everyone suggested I ask Speedo to sponsor me. But I had already spoken to Speedo in the UK and in South Africa. The brand managers said they were speaking to the person above them, but nothing ever happened. I just was not getting through to the right people.

Time was getting tight, and I had an iron in every fire I could think of. I phoned every single person I knew who had money, or knew someone with money, and I said, 'I'm about to set sail. Please would you help me?' But that elusive last bit of funding just wasn't there.

> *'Time was getting tight, and I had an iron in every fire ... but that elusive last bit of funding just wasn't there.'*

There comes a moment when you have to commit. And that moment came about a month before the departure date, when I had to buy tickets for six people to fly from London to Helsinki to the Russian port of Murmansk. I also had to buy their berths on the ship, which cost £16,500 per person. Things were getting very serious!

Hope

Everyone on the team had to take leave from their jobs. 'Lewis, are we going?' they kept asking. 'We just need one more sponsor – so we're only one decision away from going,' I told them. I had to commit, even without the money, or risk losing plane seats and the berths on the ship.

I had been training throughout that period, but the only injury I got was a repetitive strain injury from sending so many emails! I'm not joking; every morning I would wake up and start sending between 150 and 200 emails – that was on top of the phone calls for the day. No one can do this for you – no sponsorship manager or promoting agent. That's what Amundsen did, that's what Nansen did, that's what Shackleton did. They had to raise all the money themselves.

In the middle of all this I got a phone call from Talisker whisky. Now, I'm not a whisky drinker, but the folks at Talisker invited me to join a hike across the Isle of Skye. There would be two other sporting names coming along, both well-known former England and Lions rugby players: Dean Richards and Martin Bayfield. About 200 people had paid to come on this hike, sleep in tents and listen to the three of us tell stories around a fire. We would end the hike with a tasting at the Talisker distillery at Carbost.

I agreed to go along for two reasons. One, there was a small appearance fee, which I could put towards the North Pole expedition. And two, the Isle of Skye is beautiful in June and I would be able to do a cold-water swim there. And, who knows? There might be somebody on the hike who knew somebody who might want to sponsor the swim.

Bayfield is an extraordinary raconteur, and Richards had wonderful stories to tell. When it came to my turn to tell my story around the fire, I talked about my journey from Antarctica to the Isle of Skye and my dream to go to the North Pole in a month's time and to swim across it to highlight the melting of the Arctic sea ice. I told the group of hikers that I had seen the Arctic change, and that I wanted the world to take action. I wasn't a polished speaker in those days, but I spoke from the heart.

The next day, while we were having a wee dram

Hope

of Talisker (a magnificent whisky), one of the hikers walked up to me and asked, 'Have you approached Speedo?' I told him that I had been trying to get through to them for years. 'Well,' he said, 'you should speak to Stephen Rubin.' Rubin is the owner of Pentland Group, which owns a number of famous sporting brands, including Speedo. But how on earth would I get through to him?

'I used to work with him,' the man said. 'If you like, I could speak to him for you.' I thanked him, and I didn't hear from him again.

As the departure date grew near, I still believed that a miracle was going to happen. I've heard it said that there's never a shortage of money, there's only a shortage of good ideas. It's so true. If you have a good idea, someone, somewhere will want to sponsor you. And I firmly believed that this symbolic swim would get massive international coverage. I just needed the right sponsor to believe this, too. I just wasn't giving up hope.

> *'As the departure date grew near, I still believed that a miracle was going to happen.'*

— Yak 13 —

So there I was on BBC and Sky News, talking about going to the North Pole. But by three days before we were scheduled to set sail, I was beginning to sweat. Then I received a telephone call. 'Hello Lewis, It's Stephen Rubin here.' I almost dropped the phone. 'I hear you are still looking for sponsorship,' Rubin said. 'How can I help?'

I told him why I wanted to swim across the North Pole and that we were £25,000 short. 'I have children and grandchildren. I want them to see polar bears and live in a sustainable world when they grow up. I would love to support what you are doing,' he told me.

He was calling me from an airport, and was about to go on holiday. 'Email me your bank details,' he said. 'And I'll transfer the money as soon as I land.' There wasn't enough time to get to Speedo's headquarters to get kitted out, so he asked me to run down to the Covent Garden shop and get myself a Speedo swimming costume, a cap and some goggles. 'And Lewis,' he said, before he rang off, 'best of British luck to you.'

The next day I went down to the bank and put

my card in the machine; there was his deposit of £25,000. The first person I called was Professor Tim Noakes. I can still hear the Prof's triumphant shout when I told him, 'We're going to the North Pole!'

Time and time again, I've learnt that it's never over until the fat lady sings or you quit, whichever comes first. There will always be hundreds of reasons to quit, especially towards the end, when things get very tough. Think of just ONE reason to keep on going – it will make all the difference!

'Think of just ONE reason to keep on going – it will make all the difference!'

— Yak 14 —

Break

Don't be intimidated by the size of a task. Break it down into manageable pieces and start at the beginning.

They played a stirring rendition of the Russian national anthem as we sailed out of Murmansk on the icebreaker I/B *Yamal*. Most of the passengers on the ship were tourists, all excited to tick off another item on their bucket lists. We had other reasons for setting sail. We were just as excited, but to be perfectly honest I was also deep-down scared.

The seeds that germinate our dreams are sometimes planted even before we are born. In 1952, my father was assigned to monitor the first British nuclear tests, carried out on the Montebello Islands, off the coast of Western Australia. As a Royal Navy surgeon, one of his tasks was to examine all the fish killed by the blast, and to determine the amounts of radiation they had absorbed. Later, he was present at the British hydrogen bomb tests on Christmas Island in the central Pacific Ocean. I can't imagine the impact that must have had on him.

Fast forward to 1980, by which time my family was living in South Africa. That year, my father took us to the Addo Elephant National Park, near Port Elizabeth. The sight of those magnificent elephants made a profound impression on me. Every year, my father would take us to a different national park. Shortly before he died, he was determined to walk me to the top of Lion's Head, in Cape Town, to show me the beautiful proteas. His deep love of animals and plants, and of our whole environment, rubbed off on me. I was determined to carry around the world his message about the need to protect our environment.

It would take seven days to get to the North Pole. After two days, we entered the Arctic ice packs. People hung around on the upper decks looking out for polar bears, until the cold drove them back inside. As far as you could see there was nothing; we were in the middle of the Arctic Ocean. The sky was a sort of whitey grey, and the ice was white. But the water, by contrast, was completely black. I remember staring down at it and thinking that it looked like a giant inkpot with big chunks of ice floating in it.

The closer we got to the Pole, the more the excitement grew. And, as the excitement grew, my fear grew with it. Because now I could really see what I was about to get myself into.

> *'The closer we got to the Pole, the more the excitement grew. And as the excitement grew, my fear grew with it. Because now I could really see what I was about to get myself into.'*

It's 4.2km to the bottom of the Arctic Ocean. I'm not the sort of guy who is frightened of diving into the middle of the sea, although my swims usually start on land. Normally I walk into the water from a beach, and things get gradually deeper and deeper; you see the sea bed disappear beneath you and you carry on. Out here, I would be diving straight into the ocean off an ice floe, swimming a kilometre across the open sea, and getting out onto another chunk of ice. And this ocean was just so dark, so impenetrable. For some reason, there was something particularly daunting about that.

I had good reason to be scared. This sea was minus 1.7°C – colder than anything any human had ever swum in. That's 7°C colder than the water in which the *Titanic* passengers perished. Salt water freezes below zero, so you would never be able to swim in fresh water this cold. And I planned to swim one kilometre, which we estimated would take me at least 20 minutes.

> *'Salt water freezes below zero, so you would never be able to swim in fresh water this cold. And I planned to swim one kilometre, which we estimated would take at least 20 minutes.'*

When you put your mind to something, very few things are impossible to achieve. But getting your mind right can be a challenge in itself.

By the fourth day on board the *Yamal* my problem was not the cold – it was the opposite. It was just too warm for me on the ship. Every day I would go out onto the upper deck wearing just a pair of shorts and a T-shirt and try and acclimatise my body to the cold. There was a swimming pool on the ship, but for some technical reason they couldn't fill it up. And I needed to be cold and to keep fit. I was getting anxious. So on the fourth day Professor Tim Noakes pulled me aside. 'I want you to do a quick test swim,' he said.

The bleak reality hit me. 'Is this really necessary?' I asked him. Much as I wanted to acclimatise to the cold and keep fit, the prospect of diving into the middle of that dark Arctic sea no longer seemed like such a good idea. 'We are going to be at the North Pole in three days' time, what could possibly go wrong?' I should have known better than to ask that question, but I kept on trying to convince myself. 'I mean, what's the difference between 0°C, which I've swum in off Antarctica, and the temperature here?' The Prof just smiled and said, 'It's 1.7°, Lewis. That's the difference.'

I was about to discover that it was also the difference between heaven and hell, day and night, life and death.

No one had told the captain that I was aboard the ship. The look on his face when we asked him if he could stop the boat so that I could go for a quick swim was priceless! He agreed, saying he could use the opportunity to do some repairs. I suspect he just wanted to witness the spectacle ...

We knew that the final swim at the North Pole might be rushed; we didn't know what the conditions would be, and we were concerned that we might not be able to get the photographs our sponsors had asked for. So we decided to do a brief photo shoot before the test swim. The temperature was well below zero and there was an icy wind blowing. There was a lot of faffing around, quite frankly, while I stood on the ice in my Speedo swimming costume getting colder and colder. So I was already frozen before I even got into the water.

David Becker gave me the countdown – 3, 2, 1 – and I dove straight into the ink-black ocean.

It's difficult to articulate what a life-changing shock to my body it was. But I will never forget it. The difference between 0°C and minus 1.7°C is the following: when you jump into 0°C it makes you want to shout something old ladies and young children shouldn't hear. When you jump into minus 1.7°C you think, 'I am going to die very quickly. I have got to get out of here IMMEDIATELY!!' And then you panic.

My goggles fogged up and froze straight onto my face. I tore them off and tried to put them back on, but I couldn't breathe. I wasted precious seconds swallowing water and trying to fit on new goggles, while Jørgen stood on the ice shouting, 'Come on, Lewis, come *on!*' I thought: if I don't start swimming now, I am going to die in front of this Norwegian. Which was something I didn't want to do. So I put my head down and went for it.

After 50m my swimming stroke had turned into just slapping the water. The cold had gone right into my muscles and I had little control over them. And I was on fire! I was in freezing cold water, but it felt like someone had put me in a boiling cauldron. My skin was burning all over and I couldn't breathe. I just kept telling myself, 'Don't stop ...'

By the 100m mark I could feel there was something happening to my fingers. I carried on to

150m, but they were in such agony that all I could think about was Sir Ranulph Fiennes cutting his own fingers off after falling in the Arctic Ocean for just three minutes. I had never felt pain like this before. By the 200m mark it was so intense I asked Jørgen to pull me out. 'NO!' he shouted. 'You have to get to 400m.' And then he turned away and skied to the other end of the ice. This was Norwegian tough love!

I kept on going. Everyone was screaming at me. We had no support Zodiac in the water, so they were all running along the edge of the ice. When I got to 400m they pulled me out. The wind was still howling as I climbed out of the water. I screamed at Jørgen to pull my goggles off because for some reason I couldn't use my hands ... And then I saw them: my fingers had swelled to the size of sausages. The human body is 57% water, and when water freezes it expands. So the cells in my fingers had expanded and burst.

Break

I had also sliced my knee on the sharp edge of the ice, as I got out, so I started bleeding all over the place. The blood ran everywhere as it mixed with the water. Then it froze. I must have looked a sight to the tourists when I got back to the ship, but I didn't even see them. I was in absolute shock. I had never been through anything like this.

David and the Prof supported me on either side to rush me into a hot shower. It took 50 minutes under steaming water to defrost my fingers. And I still had the real swim ahead of me. If this happened after 400m, what was going to happen after a full kilometre?

That was when I realised that this swim was impossible.

The team was in shock, too. We had totally underestimated what this was going to be like. We thought it would just be 1.7°C colder. But it was exponentially more difficult.

The worst part was, I had just found my true purpose. I knew that I wanted to spend my life travelling around the world urging business and political leaders to take serious action towards protecting our oceans. There is something very wrong with us living in such a way that our children and our grandchildren won't live in a sustainable world, but in one that is devoid of the wonder and the beauty that we have known.

Now I had to ask myself, 'Are you prepared to die for this message?'

At dinner that evening, I realised that I couldn't feel my fingers because the nerves were so badly damaged. And they were so swollen that it was difficult to close them on the knife and fork.

They were no better the next morning. I needed some time alone, so after breakfast I walked to the front of the ship – a wonderful place to spot polar bears as you edge through the Arctic sea ice. It was a clear morning and utterly beautiful. But I just couldn't see a way forward.

Then I felt a tap on my shoulder. It was David Becker, who had told me four years earlier, 'Follow your own dreams, Lewis, or you'll be following someone else's.' He asked me how I was doing and I just held up my swollen hands.

He told me that the team still believed in me,

Break

and in my ability to do the swim, and that he had a plan to help get me through the distance. 'I want you to just listen,' he said. 'I'm going to give you three anchors. Between now and when we get to the North Pole, whenever you doubt yourself, whenever you think this swim is not possible, I need you to think about these three things.

'The first one is this: it is crushingly obvious that the idea of swimming a kilometre is absolutely impossible. But I know that you can swim 100m because I saw you do that yesterday. Don't think of a one-kilometre swim,' he said. 'It's too far. Just think about the 100 metres you are doing, no more.'

We had ten national flags with us, representing the nations that had played a role in this swim. 'We are going to plant a flag at every 100m mark,' he said. 'Each one will represent the people from that country who have helped you get here to do this swim. Each 100m you swim, you'll be swimming for them.'

It was a fantastic idea. Not only because it recognised the enormous contribution of all the people behind this expedition, but also because of its symbolism – wherever you are on this earth you will be impacted by what happens in the Arctic.

There were two more aspects to David's plan. The first involved going back to the beginning of my life and walking through everything that had brought me to where I was now – moments of adversity as well as moments of triumph. He asked me to picture each of my swims in vivid detail. 'When times get tough, that's exactly the moment when you need to remember all your victories,' he said. 'We are nearly at the North Pole. Remember the dozens of successful swims that brought us here.'

> *'When times get tough, that's exactly the moment when you need to remember all your victories.'*

For the final anchor, David took me to the end of my life and asked me to look back. What was the legacy I wanted to leave? Was I going to be able to look back and say that, when the time came, I stood up?

Break

'In the last two years 23% of the sea ice cover has melted away. You shouldn't be able to swim across the North Pole; it should be frozen over,' he said. 'But it isn't, and so you will swim across it, Lewis. I want you to shake the lapels of the world's leaders so they appreciate that climate change is the most pressing issue they must address.'

David had spoken to me for only about 15 minutes, but, when he'd finished, everything was different. By focusing on three anchors, he had completely changed my mindset.

I no longer believed that this swim was impossible. Instead, I had no doubt whatsoever that I was going to do it.

— Yak 15 —

Strive

The quickest way to get a job done is to do it with excellence the first time.

A few days into our journey to the North Pole, I was reminded of the lengths to which some people will go in the pursuit of excellence.

One of the members of our team was cameraman Chris Lotz. Chris's brief was, among other things, to capture images of polar bears.

Why polar bears? My North Pole swim was intended to highlight the melting of the Arctic sea ice, and the first casualties of the melting ice are polar bears, which need the ice in order to hunt for seals. Without sea ice, the polar bears will not survive. I knew that a strong image of a polar bear would communicate why I was doing this symbolic swim more than words ever could.

Now, you are not guaranteed to see a polar bear on the way to the North Pole. It takes seven days to get there, and seven days back again. And since the first two days and the last two days are through open sea, you've effectively got just 10 days in which to spot one.

Polar bears are white, and everything around you, all the way to the horizon, is white, so if you pass one on the ship, you might not even see it.

At the end of the second day, around dinnertime, I pulled Chris aside and reminded him about the polar bear images. The next day, when I came in to breakfast, Chris wasn't there. He wasn't there again for lunch, but still I didn't think anything of it because there were two sittings for each meal. But when he still wasn't there at dinner, I thought, hold on, where's Chris?

I went down to his cabin – empty. I thought he might be filming on the upper deck, but he wasn't there. I checked in the cabin of a friend he used to visit – no luck. Twenty-four hours had now passed, and I started panicking. Had he fallen overboard?

'Twenty-four hours had now passed, and I started panicking. Had Chris fallen overboard?'

I ran back to the upper deck of the ship

again and this time I looked properly, craning my head upward to take in the upper mast. And there I spotted Chris huddled behind the mast with the camera in his hand. I sprinted up two ladders to get to him, and asked him what he was doing.

'Lewis,' he said, 'inside the ship it's about 25°C. Outside it's at least minus 25°C. If I take this camera from inside the ship straight to the outside, that's a drop of 50°C, and it will mist up and possibly even break.' He'd been keeping the camera outside, wrapped in a protective tarpaulin, ready to go at a minute's notice. But that still didn't explain the missed meals. 'What if a polar bear was sighted while I was inside?' Chris said. 'It would take me precious minutes to get all my cold-weather gear on before I could come outside. I couldn't risk it. You asked me to get these pictures of a polar bear and that's what I'm doing.'

Minutes later, a pair of polar bears walked in front of the ship – a mother and her cub. They jumped off the ice

'Minutes later, a pair of polar bears walked in front of the ship – a mother and her cub.'

and swam across a patch of sea. Then the mother climbed out, with the cub not far behind her. It sprinted along after her as she disappeared into the horizon.

The entire scene took 25 minutes at most, and Chris got the whole thing, beginning to end.

We never saw another polar bear for the rest of the expedition.

That's what I understand by the pursuit of excellence. Aristotle liked to say that excellence is not an act, but a habit. Former US Secretary of State Colin Powell said that, to achieve excellence in the big things, you have to develop the habit in little matters. And when English nurse Florence Nightingale was asked the secret to her brave success, she said that she 'never gave or took any excuse'.

If you want to do a good job, the quickest and most effective way is with excellence. Because if you don't, you're going to have to go and do it again.

And you don't always get that second chance.

— Yak 16 —

Plan

Never plan for victory
and defeat in your mind
at the same time.

Three long blasts of the ship's horn signalled that we had arrived at the North Pole.

'We're here,' I thought. 'I've got to step up now.' In the three days since the test swim, I had done constant battle with negative thoughts. Every time they came up, I tried to replace them with David's three anchors. I went over the swim in my mind, again and again, visualising the minutest details, and picturing those ten flags.

After seven days at sea, everyone on the ship cheered our arrival at the Pole. I stood with the Prof on the deck and looked out over the icy vista. There were big patches of open sea and the Prof – who was 57 at the time – said, 'I wonder what this will be like in another 50 years?'

His words reminded me that there was a good reason I was doing this swim in just a Speedo swim-

> *'This wasn't some kind of stunt. This was a symbolic swim, and I needed to be courageous.'*

ming costume, cap and goggles. This wasn't some kind of stunt. This was a symbolic swim, and I needed to be courageous. When I go around the world meeting business and political leaders, I ask them to do everything they can to protect our environment. And to be courageous and ambitious about it. But there are electorates who don't want politicians to make changes, and there are boards of directors who say, 'This is going to cost too much.' If I was asking these leaders to be courageous, then I need to show courage myself. Swimming in a wetsuit or drysuit just wouldn't send the right signal.

We went down to my cabin so the Prof could strap on the chest monitor that would measure my heart rate and core body temperature. As he taped it on, I could feel his hands shaking. When one of the world's top sport scientists, and a medical doctor, gets nervous, your first thought is, 'Am I doing something very stupid here?' He was right up close to me, and I could see the emotion in his eyes.

Plan

That's when I realised what I was putting everyone through. Especially the Prof, who had sole responsibility for my safety. 'I just want you to know how very grateful I am to you today,' I told him. 'There are not many doctors who would be prepared to come all this way and assume this level of risk.'

'It's a privilege to be here, Lewis,' he replied, ever the gentleman. 'It's a historic moment. Now, let's just get this bloody swim over and done with!'

Before we went down onto the ice, I gathered my team on the ship's bridge. On a swim like this, overlap is as bad as underlap, and I needed everyone to be clear about exactly what their responsibilities were.

There were 29 people from 10 nations behind this swim, but I could only bring six of them to the North Pole. Professor Tim Noakes was doctor, David Becker was coach, Jason Roberts was photographer and fixer, Chris Lotz was cameraman, Tobie van Heerden from Investec would set out the flags, and Jørgen Amundsen was the safety guy. I started with him.

Jørgen's great-grand-uncle, the great polar explorer Roald Amundsen, used to say, 'Adventure is just bad planning.' Jørgen and I both agreed that neither of us wanted to be adventurers. Jørgen would ski next to me, motivate me, and make sure I could see the large clock he'd made especially for this swim. Every time I breathed to the right, I would be able to see exactly how how much time had passed. 'When I've finished the kilometre, you're the one who must also pull me out of the water,' I told him.

> *'Jørgen and I both agreed that neither of us wanted to be adventurers.'*

When we were deciding the order of the flags along the kilometre route, it dawned on me that the most important flag is not the first one, and not the last one, but the penultimate one, at the 900m mark. That's because things often get really tough just before the end, and that's when a lot of people quit. But the consequences of giving up at that point can be so huge. Firstly, you've wasted all that time and training. Secondly, you came so close to achieving your goal – and you quit. You'll kick yourself for the rest of your life. And thirdly

Plan

– and most importantly – quitting can so easily become a habit. While I was wondering which flag Tobie should put in there, I saw Jason grinning at me and I said, 'I'm going to put the Australian flag there, because I will never EVER give up in front of an Aussie!' Jason was delighted. The Australian photographer had also been responsible for overall logistics of the expedition. He had 25 years' experience filming in the polar regions, alongside the likes of Sir David Attenborough, so I knew he would get some magic shots.

The Prof was the person who was ultimately responsible for my safety. 'Prof Noakes is the only one who can call off this swim,' I told the team. Only one other living thing could stop us: a polar bear. We had three polar bear guards, all burly Russian soldiers just back from Chechnya, and all armed with AK-47s. 'If a curious polar bear comes along,' I told them through an interpreter, 'whatever you do, don't shoot it. That would go against everything this mission is about – we are trying to preserve polar bears and their environment!' The guard named Vladimir smiled when I told him he could beat pots and pans or do whatever else it took to turn the bears around. He was such an enormous guy; when we shook hands, it was like gripping a polar bear's paw.

We had two Zodiacs in the water. David and the Prof would be in one of them right next to me. The second boat would rove up and down to get good camera angles. Chris Lotz would be in that boat – and he had already shown that he would do whatever it took to get the footage. Finally, Jørgen would ski along the edge of the ice next to me.

There was one crucial point of business before we left the bridge. 'In the event of an accident, who is going to come in and get me?' Everyone smiled and looked to the person next to them. I imagine they were all thinking about minus 1.7°C water, and the long kilometres to the bottom. Then Jason stepped forward. 'If there is any drama, I'll come in to collect you.' Growing up in Australia, Jason had been a lifesaver, and he spoke with such conviction that I knew he really would do it. Now I had even more reason not to falter at the ninth flag.

Plan

We headed down onto the ice. Everything was set up, and the flags were standing in line. It was time to say thank you to everybody who had made this mission possible.

Some of them weren't there, but their flags stood like sentries poled into the ice. I walked the route, stopping at every one. The first one was Norway, and since Jørgen was right next to me, I could say a heartfelt thank you to him. The next flag was Sweden, then Russia, then USA and Canada. I continued down the line, thinking of all the people who had helped bring me here, from Switzerland and South Africa, from New Zealand and Australia. When I got to the final flag, I was ready.

'Let's do this,' I said to David, and I walked to the water's edge. That's when a crushing, crippling thought came into my mind: 'If things go wrong, how long will it take my frozen corpse to sink 4.2km to the bottom of the ocean?' Where that thought came from I don't know. But it's not the most empowering image to have just before trying to do the first swim across the North Pole.

I turned to David. 'If I am not looking strong,'

I said, don't let me try and do the full kilometre. Pull me out after 500m.' And right there on the ice he gave me the talking-to of my life. 'Do you know what you are doing, Lewis?!' he said, 'If you dive in there preparing to swim a kilometre, but also thinking about the possibility of getting out after just 500m, you are confusing the most important part of you – your subconscious. You can't have thoughts of victory and defeat in your mind at the same time.'

The subconscious mind can send sabotaging messages to your body. All it takes is a kernel of doubt; I needed to commit 100% to my goal. Entirely by coincidence, we had arrived at the North Pole on 15 July, the same date my father had died, a number of years earlier. I had been thinking that, if I died during the swim, I would leave my mother without her son and her husband on the same day.

'The subconscious mind can send sabotaging messages to your body. All it takes is a kernel of doubt.'

Now, David knows me very well. He knows exactly what triggers work for me. 'You see that last flag, Lewis?' he said. 'We made that last flag the British flag. Your father was British. I want you to imagine him standing beside it waiting for you.'

He told me it was time to believe in myself, to trust the team, and to carry this message: there is nothing more powerful than a made-up mind. 'Now I need you to walk up to the edge of the sea ice, to dive in, and to swim to the North Pole.'

> *He told me it was time to believe in myself, to trust the team, and to carry this message: there is nothing more powerful than a made-up mind.*

So I did.

The swim took 18 minutes and 50 seconds. And during those long freezing minutes I relived a lifetime of friendship, kinship, support and camaraderie.

They say the whole is greater than the sum of its parts. But for me, it was the individual parts that made the whole of this swim possible.

— Yak 17 —

Switch

When the path you're on stops working for you, switch to another one.

I remember the morning of 15 September 2008 very well. I had just come back from the Arctic, where I had attempted to kayak to the North Pole with Hungarian world kayaking champion Róbert Hegedüs.

Unfortunately, we hadn't got anywhere near the North Pole, and it was climate change that stopped us doing it. There had been a tremendous melt on the Alaskan side of the Arctic, and with the melt the currents pushed the ice straight towards the island of Spitsbergen, which is where we had started our expedition. So rather than being able to kayak to the Pole to demonstrate the melting ice, we were hemmed in by it.

The weeks running up to expedition had been tough. I was trying to raise funds for the trip against background murmurs of trouble in the financial markets. I started hearing terms like 'subprime mortgages', 'credit crunch' and 'regulatory failure' – concepts once limited to the realm of economics.

But we had managed to scrape the money together for the expedition. Now I was back in London, in my flat. Early that morning, I walked down to the local corner store to buy some milk and a newspaper, and there was the headline blazed across every newspaper: 'Lehman Brothers Files for Bankruptcy'.

Lehman Brothers was the fourth-largest investment bank in America. It didn't take a genius to realise how this was going to ripple around the world and impact absolutely everything.

Like so many people, on first hearing the news I felt panic. How is this going to impact me? I had put everything I had into this latest expedition. I had been dating Antoinette for some time and was planning to ask her to marry me. How would I propose to her if I couldn't even afford a ring?

For months afterwards, if you put on the television or the radio in the UK, it was just doom and gloom. It was as if they were saying, 'Will the last person to leave England please turn out the lights!'

I had swum in the Antarctic and across the North Pole. I was just gaining my voice as an advocate of the world's oceans. Would this dream be shattered because of the credit crunch? Would I have to go back to being a maritime lawyer sitting behind a desk, that is, assuming I could even find a job in that economic climate?

> *'I had just swum in the Antarctic and across the North Pole, I was just gaining my voice as an advocate of the world's oceans. Would this dream be shattered because of the credit crunch?'*

In a recession, maritime lawyers are among the first to be hit. When times get tough, trade slows down and ships don't sail. Excess tonnage is mothballed, which means less work for lawyers. Welcome to the real world.

At the time I had three sponsors: Investec, Speedo and Villemont, which made luxury watches. The Investec deal came up for renewal and was so substantially reduced that my team advised me not to take it. Speedo just sponsored my expeditions, so how could I raise the money to do the day-to-day campaigning if everybody was battening down the hatches? And then Villemont went under.

It was a frightening position to be in. I had trouble sleeping at night. When I went to the shops to buy food, I bought the bare essentials. Nothing more. What was I going to do? There was a freeze on absolutely everything – except food retailing. It was one of the few sectors that still had cash. People have got to eat.

The year before, I had visited South Africa and done a speech for the leadership team of supermarket retailer Pick n Pay, a chain which does a great deal of good work in South African communities. After the talk I met Bronwen Rohland, who was in charge of sustainability and marketing. 'You really must come talk to the schools in South Africa,' she said. 'Your dual message about protecting the environment and following your dreams in life is really important. It will resonate with our children.'

I thought it was a lovely idea, but I was in the middle of planning the kayak trip to the North Pole and I was very much a novice at public speaking. So I returned to the UK, thinking that it might be something for the future.

That future arrived with the credit crunch. Suddenly, a school tour seemed like a spot of sunshine amid the prevailing gloom. So I called Bronwen. 'Let's do this,' I said. It was a case of right place, right time, but it could have been very different.

When I arrived in Cape Town, Bronwen put me in touch with André Nel, who would structure the programme as part of the Pick n Pay School's Club, which provides much-needed support to South African schools. We set up dates at 50 schools in Cape Town, Port Elizabeth, Johannesburg and Durban. The schools were a mix of different socio-economic, religious and cultural backgrounds. We had a full schedule; three speeches a day, four days a week. We would start with a school in Cape Town.

Back in London, I had prepared what I

thought was a fantastic PowerPoint presentation. It had pictures of the North Pole and polar bears, and facts and figures about protecting the environment. I had practised it over and over in my flat.

The first school was in a depressed area of the Cape Flats rife with gangs. As we drove in, there were unemployed people on every street corner, and burnt-out cars by the side of the road. When I walked into the school hall and started to set up, I realised that I was totally unprepared. The school hall didn't have blinds, so the room was too bright to see the pictures on the screen. The microphone didn't work properly, and the kids were rowdy. Not all of them had school uniforms, and some of them were wearing hoodies. There was so little discipline that the headmaster struggled to get them to be quiet while I stood waiting on stage.

That first speech was a disaster. The second school was a little bit better. By the time we got

Switch

through the third school, I was absolutely exhausted. But André kept encouraging me. 'You're doing great, Lewis,' he said. 'Just keep on going.'

And that's how it went. Sometimes we had misunderstandings; at one school, instead of a room full of teenagers I found myself facing a group of six- to eight-year-olds. I felt like Kindergarten Cop.

But, as the tour progressed, we kept honing and improving the talks. And they got better and better. There were two in particular that stand out in my mind. The first was in Soweto, the scene of the historic uprising by schoolchildren in 1976. When we got to the school, we found that there was no school hall. 'Where are we going to do this?' I asked the principal. He pointed to a nice shady tree outside.

So much for PowerPoint. There I was, with 200 kids in front of me and nothing to show them. So I would just have to paint the pictures with words.

The only way I could describe a polar bear, which they'd certainly never seen, was to compare it to something like a lion. So I became the lion, walking around in front of them. Their eyes widened. I told them to imagine its huge paws, its enormous chest and its wild mane. A lion weighs anything from 150 to 250kg. 'Now imagine a polar bear,' I told them, stretching as tall as I could and reaching my fingers straight up. 'A big polar bear weighs up to 700kg and is 3m tall when it stands up!' I told them about how the polar bear is white, and the snow and the ice are all white, so that you don't know a polar bear is there until he's on top of you!

Nothing, not even a leaf, stirred under that tree. But, as soon as I finished the talk, hands shot up. The kids had a hundred questions. I'd learnt the first lesson of public speaking: drop the PowerPoint. Tell a story. It's the best way to get a message across. Everyone loves a story. When I left, they crowded around me so tightly that I could not move. It was underneath that tree in the middle of Soweto that I began to learn the craft of public speaking.

Our last speech of the tour was at the Inanda Seminary, an all-girls school in a bustling township outside Durban. A number of government ministers had come through this beautiful mission school, which was a world away from the Cape Flats where my tour had started. The girls all lined up in their uniforms to greet me. And then they started singing. I had to hold my tears back; for anyone of Welsh descent, music and singing is everything, and these young Zulu girls were singing with all their hearts, swaying to the rhythm as they sang.

I gave what felt like the perfect speech, right from my heart – because they had connected me with that heart. After 50 speeches, I felt like I had seen Africa through the eyes of all the children I had met. It was the most enriching experience imaginable.

'After 50 speeches, I felt like I had seen Africa through the eyes of all the children I had met. It was the most enriching experience.'

Not long after that tour, I was invited to give a speech in Rhode Island for the Business Information Forum (BIF). This was a high-tech conference for web designers and social media experts.

— Yak 17 —

All these people were talking about this app and that app, all of which went way over my head. So I thought, I'm going to speak to them like an African. And that's what I did. Africa has an oral tradition, and Africans love storytelling. They are superb at it. If you think about it, telling stories is how humans have connected with each other since time immemorial.

The speech was filmed and put online, and I was delighted when it was voted one of the seven most inspiring speeches on the internet.

At the end of that speech, a man walked up to me and asked, 'Why don't you speak at the TED (Technology, Entertainment and Design) Conference?' Now, TED was just beginning to take off then, but already it featured the very best speakers in the world, talking about ideas that change the world. 'That would be wonderful,' I said. 'But ...' Before I could tell him that TED was in another league, he said, 'Listen, my name is Richard Saul Wurman, and I *started* TED!'

So I was invited to speak at the main TED-Global Conference in Oxford. There I stood on the stage that was also hosting Prime Minister Gordon Brown, actor Stephen Fry, comedian Rory Bremner and renowned philosopher Alain de Botton. I was nervous; kids in Soweto were one thing, but this was an intimidating crowd. However TED is all about storytelling. So I just spoke from the heart again. There was a lengthy standing ovation and the talk went viral on the internet.

I did my TED talk in July. Shortly afterwards, I started getting calls from blue-chip companies around the world like Unilever, Microsoft, Mercedes-Benz and Ernst & Young, asking me to come talk to them. Soon I was doing over 120 speeches a year.

The more talks I did, the more I realised that CEOs and business leaders are, with respect, just the same as kids in a township seminary or a Cape Flats school. They are easily distracted. They are busy and under pressure, so you've got to go in there and grab them, and tell them a story like an African. And, most importantly, make sure you have finished speaking before they have finished listening! Keep it short. Keep it tight. No waffle.

I had to take the stories of the Antarctic and the North Pole and make them meaningful and relevant to their businesses and their lives.

I realised something else, too. Out of the worst thing that could have happened, the thing that nearly crushed me, came the best thing in the world.

> *'Out of the worst thing that could have happened, the thing that nearly crushed me, came the best thing in the world.'*

I know many people have lost their jobs and their homes because of the global financial crisis, and it has caused untold hardship. But it forced me to find a new way to earn an income and be an ocean advocate. Now, every single week, I was talking to people about protecting our oceans – and talking to the very leaders who could make the changes that are required. I was doing 120 speeches a year, which meant there was no need for any sponsors. It felt like I had 120!

Complacency is a terrible thing. It can soften your focus and keep you in a rut. There's nothing like change to force you out of complacency. I had learned an important lesson: don't put all your eggs in one basket, because times can change, and you need to be able to change with them.

By changing my focus, I saw a side of Africa that I might never have seen, and was connected with the warmth and the beauty of its people.

— Yak 18 —

Trust

Trust your gut – especially when it comes to risks.

It probably goes without saying that nobody has ever walked up Mount Everest with a boat. At least, not before we did it, with the help of a couple of yaks and a decoy.

Why on earth would we do such a thing? Because we needed to take a support boat up to Lake Pumori, a glacial lake in which we were attempting to complete the world's highest swim.

Safety is a big issue with any long-distance swim. When something goes wrong in swimming, it happens quickly. There have been Channel crossings where the swimmer was moving along just fine and then suddenly disappeared, sunk and gone to the bottom of the English Channel before the support crew even realised what had happened.

This was one of the concerns Professor Tim Noakes had when I was swimming across the

— Yak 18 —

North Pole. The water there is completely black, and very deep; if I went under, there was nothing they could do to find my body. So I was either going to wear a harness, or the Prof was going to make sure the support team was right next to me in a boat. He chose the latter option.

We wanted to put the same safety measures in place on Everest. The problem with a glacial lake is that glacial water is often milky blue; on Everest it was an opaque blue mixed with brown, and you couldn't see through it at all. I knew that if I went under, they wouldn't be able to find me. So we were going to have to have a boat next to me. And that meant taking one 5,200m up the mountain – that's nearly the height of Mount Kilimanjaro.

When you start to think about the logistics of getting a boat up a mountain, it can become a little overwhelming. The first question is: what type of boat? You can't drive it up on a trailer – there are no roads. Local Sherpas could not carry it. It was too heavy. So it would have to be carried on the back of a yak – big strong ox local to the region. The yaks would be climbing up steep, slippery paths, and crossing plenty of narrow suspension bridges. It would have to be as light as possible.

We also needed a boat we could deflate and dismantle, so we settled on a small inflatable dingy. We didn't need an engine, which would have been very heavy; instead, two team members would row the boat alongside me. The oars and foot pumps would be carried by a second yak.

Now, getting a yak up a mountain requires experience. They are big and they are strong, and they are often belligerent first thing in the morning. We hired a team of Sherpas to do boat detail. The Sherpas came with a span of yaks. Every morning during the two weeks of our ascent, we would wake up to the sound of the guys fighting with their yaks outside our tents. We'd hear them muttering as they tried to get the harness around the yaks' noses. The yaks always resisted because

> *'Getting a yak up a mountain requires experience. They are big and they are strong, and they are often belligerent first thing in the morning.'*

— Yak 18 —

they'd been eating all night; they were not keen to be separated from their food to start work. We'd hear the thud of the yaks hoofing those poor Sherpas, and felt very grateful to be still in our sleeping bags ...

Just before we set out, the leader of the Sherpas, Binod Rai, pulled me aside. 'What worries me is that nobody has ever taken a boat up Everest before,' he said. 'And when we walk past the rangers as we enter the national park, I can imagine them not knowing what to do. And then they will insist on calling an official in Kathmandu and that will just tie us up.' We had hit a potential snag involving my pet hate: red tape.

Binod's father had been a Gurkha officer in the British Army, and military-style strategising was clearly in his blood. 'What we need,' he said, 'is something that distracts their attention. While they are fiddling with that, we'll just walk casually past with our boat.'

I liked his thinking. And what better way to distract attention from a boat than with another, more obvious, boat? We managed to rustle up a kayak – one of those big red plastic tubs. It was just a little bit taller than I am, and it was heavy. But man for man, pound for pound, I have never met any people stronger than the Nepalese Sherpas. Our boat decoy, Phurba Sherpa, strapped the boat on his back by tying one end of a rope around the kayak, and the other around his head. And then he started walking up the mountain. It was backbreaking work, for which I was exceptionally grateful. And, sure enough, when he got to the park entrance, he was stopped by incredulous park rangers.

Meanwhile, our real support boat was waiting about a kilometre back, heavily disguised under a tarpaulin. Phurba Sherpa had a mobile phone, and instructions to call us as soon as he was stopped. When he did, we urged him to start arguing with the officials, and to keep them busy until the rest of us had passed the rangers and made a good distance up the mountain.

> *'Meanwhile, our real support boat was heavily disguised and strapped under a tarpaulin.'*

— Yak 18 —

It all went perfectly according to plan, to the relief of everyone – even poor Phurba Sherpa, who had to turn around with the kayak on his back and walk for a whole week all the way back down the mountain.

We had our boat, but we didn't even put it in the water for the test swim at Lake Imja, a glacial lake on the slopes of Lhotse. It was only a short swim, and so we thought, 'What could possibly go wrong swimming close to the edge of the lake?' Nothing went wrong, but that was not the case when we climbed up onto Everest. The effect of the extra altitude was brutal. We made damn sure we had that boat inflated and riding right next to me during the main swim.

That swim is another story. But here's the moral of this one: safety always comes first, and preparation is a crucial part of that.

Fail to prepare, and be prepared to fail. But if you've done your preparation thoroughly, you can trust your safety measures, you can trust your team, and you can concentrate on getting the job done.

At one point during our preparation I'd been

tempted to forgo the boat. Getting it up the mountain had just seemed like too much hassle. But something told me I would need it up there, and I'm so glad I trusted my intuition. Your gut is a built-in alarm. It's there to protect you. If something does not feel right in your gut, it generally is not right. And when the altitude forced me to make a radical shift in my swimming tactics, my life depended on having that boat there.

> *'Your gut is a built-in alarm. It's there to protect you. If something does not feel right in your gut, it generally is not right.'*

Whatever it takes to get the job done, you just have to do it. If that means taking a boat up the highest mountain on earth, that's what you have to do.

And never, ever, let red tape stop you.

— Yak 19 —

Change

Just because a strategy has worked for you before doesn't mean it will work again. Be prepared to make a radical tactical shift.

Some of the best advice I ever received was never to try and bully Mount Everest. It came during my attempt to complete the world's highest-ever long-distance swim. I was in the middle of Lake Pumori, 5,200m above sea level on the slopes of Mount Everest. The lake is glacial, so the water was freezing cold, but that wasn't the problem. The problem was the altitude. This mountain was putting me in my place, and I was in trouble.

After the North Pole, I had resolved never to do another cold-water swim, but the Himalayas changed my mind. Glaciers are not just ice: they are a source of water for nearly 2 billion people. If glaciers melt away, as scientists predict they will, the people living in the lands fed by the Himalayas – including India, China, Pakistan and Bangladesh – will find themselves in conflict over water.

Yak 19

We cannot survive without water. We need it for everything.

We had heard that small lakes were forming on Mount Everest's Khumbu Glacier – the same one Sir Edmund Hillary and Tenzing Norgay crossed in 1953 en route to the summit. So we decided to head out to Nepal to swim across one of them and bring attention to the issue of melting glaciers and the impact it could have on peace in the region.

The hike up to Everest is a life-changing walk for many people, and I would encourage everyone who has the opportunity to go to grab it with both hands. It's not just the beauty of the Himalayan peaks and glaciers, but also the generosity and kindness of the Nepalese people. As we hiked up Everest, with the help of a team of Sherpas and their woolly yaks, we couldn't help but be

> *'As we hiked up Mount Everest, with the help of a team of Sherpas and their woolly yaks, we couldn't help but be star-struck. But for me, the harsh beauty of the terrain brought other concerns.'*

Change

star-struck. But, for me, the harsh beauty of the terrain brought other concerns.

If you compete in a big international sporting event like the Olympics, you know exactly what you are training for. You know exactly when you are going to be competing, and in what conditions, so you can be in peak condition on the day.

When you are preparing for Everest, you don't know when, or if, you are going to be able to perform. You don't know when the conditions are going to be right, you don't know how sick you are going to be from the altitude. And every day you are on the mountain your condition is deteriorating. It's a very different game.

This time I wasn't just swimming in freezing water, I was swimming at high altitude. This combination had never been attempted before. Whenever we came to a river on the way up the mountain, I submerged myself in it for a few minutes to adapt to the cold. In terms of altitude, we climbed very slowly. I just had to hope my body would acclimatise in time for the swim.

Shortly before we came to Mount Everest itself, we took a detour to Lake Imja. The lake is about 2km long and one kilometre wide. It leaves a deep impression on you when you look out over a lake and realise that just 40 years ago there was a massive glacier in its place.

I did a test swim here, staying close to the edge so we wouldn't have to use our boat. I swam for about six minutes – the water was 2°C – with no problems at all. After that, we were ready to head up Everest and find Lake Pumori.

Now, Imja wasn't my only preparation for the swim. Earlier in the year I had travelled to the Andes, and done some training in Laguna del Diamante (Diamond Lake), at 3,200m above sea level, near the Chilean–Argentinian border. Imja was at 5,000m, so Pumori didn't seem prohibitive at 5,200m. But what a difference 200m makes.

I prepared to do that swim the same way I've done every cold-water swim for the last 23 years: dive in and go for it with everything I've got. That's the way I'd swum around Robben Island and the North Cape, and across the North Pole. That's the way I'd swum in the Andes and in Imja. Every time

Change

I got cold, I just swam faster and harder. So when David Becker gave me the countdown, I dived in and started speeding across Lake Pumori.

About 50m in, I realised something was very wrong. I was gasping for air. I began choking, and soon I had no strength in my body at all. I tried treading water and couldn't even hold my head above the water. I sank to the bottom of the lake.

Luckily, it was a very shallow lake, so I was able to push myself up again and take a couple of deep breaths. I tried to continue with a few strokes of crawl but I was just spluttering away. The General motioned for me to get out immediately. 'I'm sorry, Lewis,' he said, once I was back on shore. 'You are choking and if we carry on like this you could drown. Then you will be just another person who dies on this mountain. Safety must come first.'

The mountain deaths had been vividly apparent to us on the way up. Many who die on the mountain lie there for years because they are so inaccessible. But, that year, the Nepalese government had decided to try and recover their bodies. When you are walking up a mountain to attempt something

> *'When you are walking up a mountain to attempt something that nobody's ever tried before, and you pass people bringing corpses down, it becomes very clear that if you get it wrong, the consequences could be fatal.'*

that nobody's ever tried before, and you pass people bringing corpses down, it becomes very clear that if you get it wrong, the consequences could be fatal. But I wasn't yet ready to give up.

We went back down the mountain to the village of Gorak Shep. The General called the team together and asked each person what they thought had gone right, and what had gone wrong. After that he sat me down and said, 'Lewis, I think you need to take a radical tactical shift.' I asked him what he meant. 'Why,' he replied, 'are you trying to swim so quickly?'

The answer seemed so obvious to me. I held up my hands and told him, 'I couldn't feel these for four months after the North Pole swim. I need to swim fast to generate heat.' The General just smiled at me and said, 'But Lewis, this water is warm – it's 2°C!' Then he told me the team's rec-

Change

ommendation: instead of swimming as quickly as possible, I should swim as *slowly* as possible.

Instead of swimming crawl with my head in the water all the time, he suggested I try breaststroke, which would enable me to breathe whenever I needed to. 'This is not a race, Lewis,' he reminded me. Then came the most important part: 'Instead of swimming with aggression, which worked when you were swimming around North Cape and at the North Pole, I recommend you swim with real humility.' That's when he pointed up to the highest mountain in the world and told me, 'You cannot bully Mount Everest.'

It was like the penny had dropped. I knew what I had to do. My choice was simple – change or drown.

> *'It was like the penny had dropped. I knew what I had to do. My choice was simple – change or drown.'*

We spent two more days acclimatising at Gorak Shep. I got a lot more oxygen into my body. When the day came, Sanjeev, a young Sherpa who was helping us on the mountain, called me from my tent.

Yak 19

He led the way, followed by the General, then myself, then David Becker, then the three who would man the boat – emergency doctor Shaun Gottschalk, Michael Henderson and Martin Jenkins – and finally the Sherpas and yaks carrying the boat itself.

Now we were glad we'd hauled the boat all the way up the mountain. Up to this point, we had been reluctant to take the boat out, and assemble it, not just because it was a hassle, but because we were concerned that we might be breaking some park rules. Now we had no qualms about it whatsoever. Safety first.

By the time we reached the lake the fear was like a fist in my stomach. I was thinking, 'If I go too quickly I'm going to drown. If I go too slowly I could lose my fingers. I've got to get my speed just right.'

That's when Sanjeev pulled me aside. 'Come and lie down here on this rock,' he

> *'I was thinking, "If I go too quickly I'm going to drown. If I go too slowly I could lose my fingers. I've got to get my speed just right."'*

said. He and two other Sherpas lit some incense and said some prayers. It was a clear day and I could see the teams leaving Everest Base Camp on their way to the highest point on Earth. It was very, very peaceful.

After a while, I stood up, shook everyone's hands, slowly got into the water and slowly started swimming across this lake.

I swam 250m and there was no problem. I swam another 250m, and still no problem. I almost felt like I was cheating, because it was so easy. At 600m I was feeling the cold, at 650m my fingers were starting to freeze. At 700m I felt colder than I was when I climbed out of the sea at the North Pole. When we got to 750m, I was so cold I thought I must break into crawl and finish these last 250m as quickly as possible. That's when I heard Sanjeev shouting out, 'Slower, Lewis, SLOWER!' Luckily, I listened to him. Those last slow 250m were some of the most painful of my life.

We learnt two crucial lessons on Mount Everest. The first was that just because something has worked very successfully in the past doesn't mean it will necessarily work in the future.

The second lesson was also about change. It is this: you can change your stroke, you can change your speed, but for real and effective change to take place you have to completely change your mindset.

And when you do that, absolutely anything is possible.

— Yak 20 —

Stand Up

If it doesn't feel right,
stand up and fix it.

There come moments in your life when you need to stand up.

For my father, it was during the Second World War, when he joined the Royal Navy. For his uncles, it was during the First World War, when they went off to serve in the trenches. They were courageous men and they responded to the call of their time.

But there's a different kind of courage involved in choosing to go against the popular tide. Do you go along with the masses or stand up for what you think is right?

The announcement by Shell that it wished to explore for shale gas, by way of hydraulic fracturing, or fracking, in South Africa's Karoo was one of those moments for me.

While many South Africans were excited by

the promise of new jobs, I believed that this major energy company was spearheading something that was very, very wrong.

And why would we want this kind of technology in South Africa? In the United States, fracking has contaminated aquifers and scarred the landscape. Why would we want to use up all the fossil fuels and accelerate climate change? Why would we want to damage our water supply? Especially in the Karoo – the Afrikaans word *karo* is thought come from a Khoikhoi word for 'thirsty land'.

What's more, this was being proposed in an area that I had loved so much as a child, an area where my cousins farm – and have been farming since 1820. Some of my ancestors are buried there. If I was not to defend this, what would I defend?

There was a public hearing planned in Cape Town in March 2011. The board of Shell (South Africa) was going to be there, explaining why they thought fracking should be allowed. I asked them whether I could present my views, and they agreed.

So I stood up there. And this is what I said:

Stand Up

Ladies and gentlemen, thank you for the opportunity to address you. My name is Lewis Pugh.

This evening, I want to take you back to the early 1990s in this country. You may remember them well.

Nelson Mandela had been released. There was euphoria in the air. However, there was also widespread violence and deep fear. This country teetered on the brink of a civil war. But somehow, somehow, we averted it. It was a miracle!

And it happened because we had incredible leaders. Leaders who sought calm. Leaders who had vision. So in spite of all the violence, they sat down and negotiated a New Constitution.

I will never forget holding the Constitution in my hands for the first time. I was a young law student at the University of Cape Town. This was the cement that brought peace to our land. This was the document which held our country together. The rights contained in it made us one.

I remember thinking to myself – never again will the Rights of South Africans be trampled upon.

Now every one of us, every man and every women – black, white, coloured, Indian, believer and non-believer – has the right to vote. We all have the Right to Life. And our children have the right to a basic education. These rights are enshrined in our Constitution.

These rights were the dreams of Oliver Tambo. These rights were the dreams of Nelson Mandela. These rights were the dreams of Mahatma Gandhi, of Desmond Tutu and of Molly Blackburn. These rights were our dreams.

People fought – and died – so that we could enjoy these rights today.

Also enshrined in our Constitution, is the Right to a Healthy Environment and the Right to Water. Our Constitution states that we have:

'the Right to have our environment protected for the benefit of our generation and for the benefit of future generations.'

Fellow South Africans, let us not dishonour these rights. Let us not dishonour those men and women who fought and died for these rights. Let us not allow corporate greed to disrespect our Constitution and desecrate our environment.

Never, ever did I think that there would be a debate in this arid country about which was more important – gas or water. We can survive without gas. We cannot live without water.

> 'Never, ever did I think that there would be a debate in this arid country about which was more important – gas or water. We can survive without gas. We cannot live without water.'

If we damage our limited water supply – and fracking will do just that – we will have conflict again here in South Africa. Look around the world. Wherever you damage the environment, you have conflict.

Fellow South Africans, we have had enough conflict in this land – now is the time for peace.

A few months ago I gave a speech with the former President of Costa Rica. Afterwards I asked him, 'Mr President, how do you balance the demands of development against the need to protect the environment?'

He looked at me and said, 'It is not a balancing act. It is a simple business decision. If we cut down our forests in Costa Rica to satisfy a timber company, what will be left for our future?'

But he pointed out, 'It is also a moral decision. It would be morally wrong to chop down our forests and leave nothing for my children and my grandchildren.'

Ladies and gentlemen, that is what is at stake here today: our children's future. And that of our children's children.

There may be gas beneath our ground in the Karoo. But are we prepared to destroy our environment for 5 to 10 years' worth of fossil fuel and further damage our climate?

Yes, people will be employed – but for a short while. And when the drilling is over, and Shell have packed their bags and disappeared, then what? Who will be there to clean up? And what jobs will our children be able to eke out?

Now, Shell will tell you that their intentions are honourable. That fracking in the Karoo will not damage our environment. That they will not contaminate our precious water. That they will bring jobs to South Africa. That gas is clean and green. And that they will help secure our energy supplies.

When I hear this – I have one burning question. Why should we trust them? Africa is to Shell what the Gulf of Mexico is to BP.

Shell, you have a shocking record here in Africa. Just look at your operations in Nigeria. You have spilt more than 9 million barrels of crude oil into the Niger Delta. That's twice the amount of oil that BP spilt into the Gulf of Mexico.

You were found guilty of bribing Nigerian

officials – and to make the case go away in America, you paid an admission of guilt fine of US$48 million.

And to top it all, you stand accused of being complicit in the execution of Nigeria's leading environmental campaigner Ken Saro-Wiwa and eight other activists.

If you were innocent, why did you pay US$15.5 million to their widows and children to settle the case out of court?

Shell, the path you want to take us down is not sustainable. I have visited the Arctic for seven summers in a row. I have seen the tundra thawing. I have seen the retreating glaciers. And I have seen the melting sea ice. I have seen the impact of global warming from the Himalayas all the way down to the low-lying Maldive Islands. Wherever I go, I see it.

Now is the time for change. We cannot drill our way out of the energy crisis. The era of fossil fuels is over. We must invest in renewable

'We must invest in renewable energy. And we must not delay!'

energy. And we must not delay!

Shell, we look to the north of our continent and we see how people got tired of political tyranny. We have watched as despots, who have ruled ruthlessly year after year, have been toppled in a matter of weeks.

We too are tired. Tired of corporate tyranny. Tired of your short-term, unsustainable practices.

We watched as Dr Ian Player, a game ranger from Natal, and his friends, took on Rio Tinto (one of the biggest mining companies in the world) and won.

And we watched as young activists from across Europe brought you down to your knees, when you tried to dump an enormous oil rig into the North Sea.

Shell, we do not want our Karoo to become another Niger Delta.

Do not underestimate us. Goliath can be brought down. We are proud of what we have achieved in this young democracy – and we are not about to let your company come in and destroy it.

So let this be a Call to Arms to everyone across South Africa, who is sitting in the shadow of Goliath: stand up and demand these fundamental human rights promised to you by our Constitution. Use your voices – tweet, blog, petition, rally the weight of your neighbours and of people in power. Let us speak out from every hilltop. Let us not go quietly into this bleak future.

Let me end off by saying this – You have lit a fire in our bellies, which no man or woman can extinguish. And if we need to, we will take this fight all the way from your petrol pumps to the very highest Court in this land. We will take this fight from the farms and towns of the Karoo to the streets of London and Amsterdam. And we will take this fight to every one of your shareholders. And I have no doubt that, in the end, good will triumph over evil.

I titled that speech 'Standing up to Goliath'. The next day it was printed verbatim in a number of newspapers. Every generation will be asked to stand up for something. Desmond Tutu was asked to stand up. Nelson Mandela was asked to stand up. But this is not just about great people; it's about ordinary folk like you and me.

If you are not prepared to stand up and fight for water, the most basic human need, what are you prepared to stand up for?

Some of the greatest injustices in history happened because good men and women kept quiet. As this book goes to print in South Africa, the one-year moratorium on prospecting has ended, and government is considering issuing licences to prospect for gas in the Karoo.

And again I urge all South Africans to stand up.

— Yak 21 —

Dream

It's never too late to pursue your dreams – just make sure you are in the right place to achieve them.

I was born in Plymouth, in the southwest of England, and spent my early childhood between that town and nearby Tavistock, the birthplace of Sir Francis Drake.

Whenever I walked down to the local post office, I would walk past the statue of Sir Francis. He stood proudly next to a globe, reminding passersby that he was the first Englishman to sail around the world.

My dad was a prolific writer who always sent a lot of letters, and I was the one who posted them for him. So I walked past that statue often. Although I knew nothing about what it must have taken Sir Francis Drake to achieve what he did, my seven-year-old self started to imagine what it would be like to circumnavigate the globe.

When Sir Francis Drake sailed around the Cape

of Good Hope, he described it as the 'Fairest Cape in the whole circumference of the Earth'. I didn't know it then, but many years later that Fairest Cape would become my home.

Cape Town has been a popular shipping stop since Sir Francis's time, and even more so today. Shipping is a tight industry, and its margins became even narrower after the global financial crisis. Many ships were mothballed; others sail without insurance. Those are often the ones that can't afford the private security needed to safely pass the pirates lying in wait off the Horn of Africa. So they sail around the Cape instead.

This is not good news for local marine life.

On 8 September 2009, the bulk carrier MV *Seli 1* ran aground during a heavy winter storm off Cape Town's Dolphin Beach. She was carrying coal.

The Cape of Good Hope was also called the Cape of Storms, because of the wild winds and high seas that rage there. So the salvage companies in Cape Town have plenty of experience rescuing ships. Tugs were sent to the *Seli 1*, but they arrived too late. To make matters worse, the ship's Turkish owners had allowed their hull insurance to lapse. They didn't have the money for salvage, so they simply abandoned her.

While local and national government argued about who was going to pay for the removal, the *Seli 1* lodged deeper into the sand. Salvors removed the coal and most of the bunker oil, but there was still some left in the hull. When the next big storm came through, it broke the ship's back and spilt oil everywhere.

'When the next big storm came through, it broke the ship's back and spilt oil everywhere.'

The *Seli 1* sat there for the better part of three years. With every storm, more oil was released into the sea. The oil spread along the coast from Dolphin Beach to Blouberg Beach and covered one of the main feeding grounds of the African penguin, a species that is only found off the coasts of South Africa and Namibia.

That was when I became involved with the Southern African Foundation for the Conservation of Coastal Birds (SANCCOB), a non-profit rescue centre that rehabilitates penguins and other sea birds.

SANCCOB is headed by Margaret Roestorf and staffed almost entirely by volunteers. Coincidentally, a number of them are students from my home town; Plymouth University sends students for practical experience during their second and third years of study.

A penguin researcher once told me that penguins all have distinct personalities, just like humans. Some are dozy, some are happy, some are grumpy, some of them are thieves – stealing rocks to make nests – and all of them have sharp beaks! As an Ambassador of SANCCOB, I invited the British High Commissioner to South Africa, Dame Nicola Brewer, to come and see what was happening at

Dream

the SANCCOB rescue centre following the *Seli 1* spill and to meet the British students. Dame Nicola pulled on Wellington boots and plastic overalls and got stuck in helping to feed the penguins. It seemed as if she got all the grumpy ones that day, but she was a good sport about it.

While we were there, Margaret shared some statistics about the African penguin that stopped us in our tracks. 'We've seen a 64% decrease in African penguins in just ten years,' she said. 'In the 1900s there were between three and four million penguins. At the turn of the millennium their numbers had plummeted to just 100,000. Today there are only 60,000. If we carry on like this, they will soon be extinct.' The thing about penguins is that they are an indicator species. Because penguins don't fly, scientists can count them pretty accurately, and their numbers tell us what is happening to other species.

I called Emily Lewis-Brown, a friend of mine who is a marine biologist in London, and asked her if this rapid decline in species numbers was reflected elsewhere. 'Lewis,' she said, 'if you go to the Great Barrier Reef, if you go to the Red Sea, the Mediterranean, the North Sea, or the Arctic Ocean, you will see an enormous decrease in marine birds, and in fish. Our oceans are under threat like never before.'

I made a decision right there that I had to do something about it. I had to join the dots between the Great Barrier Reef, the Red Sea, the Mediterranean, the North Sea and the Arctic Ocean. I began to dream of seeing protected areas declared in the most fragile parts of our oceans.

It's a dream shared by many people, and it involves governments declaring marine protected areas or aquatic national parts all over the world and policing them. If we've created national parks on land, why can't we do the same in the sea? Over 10% of terrestrial earth is protected, yet less than 2% of our oceans are protected. Now is the time to change that.

I know that marine protected areas on their own will not stop climate change, or overfishing, or pollution. But imagine a world where the most beautiful and environmentally sensitive parts of our oceans are protected. That will be a real advance

Dream

towards a future in which our marine biodiversity, which is so crucial to all life on earth, is protected.

It's not a small dream. But if there's one thing I know about dreams it's this: it's much easier to achieve big dreams than it is small ones. Big dreams require big passion. And when you've got passion it's easier to inspire others to come along and help you.

I've been swimming for 25 years, and I don't think there is one swim that I have done where someone didn't say beforehand, 'I don't think it's possible' or 'You'll never make it'. If someone tells you that you can't achieve your dream, don't waste good time arguing. Walk away and do it.

> *'If someone tells you that you can't achieve your dream, don't waste good time arguing. Walk away and do it.'*

And it's also never too late to start fulfilling your dreams. As this book goes to print, Otto Thaning, now 72 years old, is planning to be the oldest person to swim the English Channel. When he tried it with me in 1992, he failed because of bad conditions. He tried again in 1993 and spent three weeks at Dover waiting for a good day, which never came. But he's no quitter. He returned in 1994 and made it. When he finished, he said to me, 'I really enjoyed that! If I keep my good health then I'm going to have another go at it in my 70s.' And now he is.

When you have a dream or purpose in life, it keeps you going. And just as it's never to late to start fulfilling your dream, it's also never too early. If you want to swim the Channel, get down to your local pool and start swimming. Don't look for other people to validate your dreams. If it feels right, just go for it.

> *'When you have a dream or purpose in life, it keeps you going. And just as it's never too late to start fulfilling your dream, it's also never too early. Don't look for other people to validate your dreams. If it feels right, just go for it.'*

The key is to keep striving, to keep pushing, and to not sit back. Keep focused and don't get distracted. If I'm going to persuade heads of state and governments to create marine-protected areas

Dream

around the world, I'm going to have to circumnavigate the globe to do it. And isn't that what I've always dreamed of?

I've used swimming to carry a message about our environment. There is nothing more symbolic than swimming across a patch of sea that used to be frozen over, but is now open water because of climate change. I always want my next expedition to be even more challenging, and more symbolic, and to generate more attention around the issue.

The mission I'm planning as we go to print is my most ambitious yet. Watch this space …

Timeline

Year	Event
1969	Born on 5 December in Plymouth, England.
1980	Moves to Grahamstown, South Africa.
1987	Swims from Robben Island to Cape Town (7km), in 3 hours.
1990	Reads Law and Politics at the University of Cape Town (5 years).
1992	Completes first swim across Lake Malawi (25km), in 9 hours 52 minutes.
	Swims across the English Channel (35km), in 14 hours 50 minutes.
1993	Breaks record for fastest swim from Dassen Island to Yzerfontein (10km), in 2 hours 35 minutes.
	Father dies on 15 July, aged 72.
1994	Completes first swim around Cape Agulhas, the most southerly point in Africa (10km), in 4 hours 1 minute.
1998	Returns to England.
	Joins Ince & Co, a maritime law firm in London.
	Joins the British Army as a reservist in 21 Special Air Service.

Timeline

1999   Reads for a Master's degree in International Law at Cambridge University.

2000   Joins Stephenson Harwood law firm in London.

2003   Completes first swim around the North Cape, the most northerly point in Europe (5km), in 1 hour 4 minutes.

2004   Completes first swim around the Cape of Good Hope, South Africa (12km), in 3 hours 15 minutes.

Completes first staged swim around the Cape Peninsula (100km) from the V&A Waterfront to Muizenberg, in 13 days.

Breaks record for fastest swim around Robben Island (10km), in 3 hours 42 minutes.

Completes first staged swim down Norway's Sognefjord, the longest unfrozen fjord in the world (204km), in 21 days.

2005   Completes the world's most northerly long-distance swim across Magdalenefjord, Spitsbergen. The 1km swim, in 3°C water, takes 21 minutes.

12 hours later, breaks that record with a 1km swim, in 3°C water, around Verlegenhuken, Spitsbergen, in 20 minutes and 30 seconds.

Completes the most southerly long-distance swim at Petermann Island, Antarctica. The 1km swim, in 0°C water, takes 18 minutes.

Completes a 1.6km swim across Whaler's Bay in Deception Island, South Shetland Islands. The swim takes 30 minutes and 30 seconds.

2006   Swims across Nelson Mandela Bay in South Africa

Timeline

(16km), in 4 hours 57 minutes.

Completes first swim from Manly Beach through the Sydney Heads to the Sydney Opera House (16km), in 6 hours 1 minute.

Becomes the first person to complete the 'Holy Grail of Swimming' – a long-distance swim in every ocean of the world.

Wins gold medal in the 500m freestyle at the World Winter Swimming Championships in Finland.

Breaks world record for longest swim in ice water (just above 0°C) – 1,250m in Nigards Glacier Lake, Norway.

During a severe drought, completes the first staged swim down the River Thames (350km), in 21 days, to highlight the impact of climate change.

Joins the Council of Ambassadors of the World Wide Fund for Nature (WWF) in the UK.

2007 Completes first staged swim across the width of the low-lying Maldive Islands (140km), in 10 days, to draw attention to the impact of rising sea levels.

Completes first swim across the North Pole to highlight the impact of melting sea ice. The 1km swim, in water measuring minus 1.7°C, takes 18 minutes and 50 seconds.

2008 Attempts to kayak across the Arctic Ocean to the North Pole with Hungarian paddler Róbert Hegedüs. The expedition was abandoned after failing to find a route through the sea ice.

2009 Undertakes a tour of South African schools to talk about protecting the environment.

Timeline

The MV *Seli 1*, a Turkish bulk carrier, runs aground off Cape Town. During the following three winters, oil trapped in the wreck kills many sea birds. Lewis becomes an Ambassador for SANCCOB, the NGO that cleans and rehabilitates oiled sea birds.

Marries his childhood sweetheart, Antoinette Malherbe.

Awarded South Africa's highest honour – the Order of Ikhamanga (Gold Class).

2010 Completes first swim on Mount Everest, in a glacial lake, to highlight the melting of the glaciers in the Himalayas. The 1km swim, at an altitude of 5,200m, takes 22 minutes and 51 seconds.

Appointed a Young Global Leader by the World Economic Forum.

2011 After Shell announces plans to explore for gas in the Karoo using hydraulic fracturing (fracking), Lewis delivers a speech entitled 'Standing up to Goliath' to a packed crowd in Cape Town.

Appointed a Fellow of the Royal Geographical Society in London.

Gives a speech with Archbishop Desmond Tutu at the opening of the UN Climate Change Conference (COP17) in Durban.

2012 Lewis works with SANCCOB to develop a contingency plan to clean and rehabilitate seabirds from future oil spills in the sub-Antarctic region.

2013 Inducted into the International Marathon Swimming Hall of Fame.

Appointed 'Patron of the Oceans' by the United Nations Environment Programme.

Temperatures

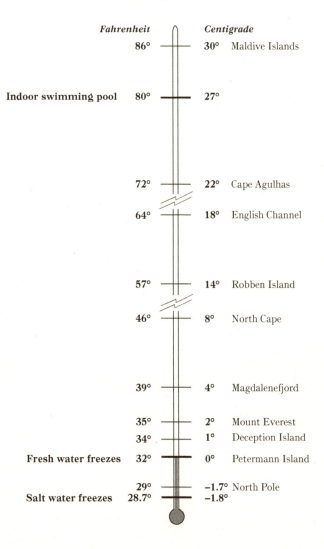

	Fahrenheit		Centigrade	
	86°		30°	Maldive Islands
Indoor swimming pool	80°		27°	
	72°		22°	Cape Agulhas
	64°		18°	English Channel
	57°		14°	Robben Island
	46°		8°	North Cape
	39°		4°	Magdalenefjord
	35°		2°	Mount Everest
	34°		1°	Deception Island
Fresh water freezes	32°		0°	Petermann Island
	29°		−1.7°	North Pole
Salt water freezes	28.7°		−1.8°	

Thanks

The swims, the expeditions, the campaigns to highlight the vulnerability of our oceans, and the opportunity to realise my dreams were only possible because *many* good people helped me. Their generosity was appreciated at the time and I remember each one again in alphabetical order.

With much gratitude to: **Roman Abramovich**, but for whom I might still be marooned on a tropical island in the Indian Ocean; **Jørgen Amundsen**, for skiing next to me across the North Pole; **Chris Anderson**, for polishing my TED speech; **Richard Armstrong**, for guiding me to France; **Peter Aspden**, for your generous words; my geography teacher **Ted Baker**, for inspiring me with stories of sailing to distant lands; **Peter Bales**, for helping me with my early swims; **David Becker**, the most wonderful and generous friend one could ever have; **Simon Blackburn**, who toughened me up in the freezing waters of the Skeleton Coast; former Prime Minister **Tony Blair**, whose intervention kept the overzealous harbourmaster at bay; the men of the British **Special Air Service** (SAS), keep safe wherever you may be; **Dame Nicola Brewer**, for feeding some very hungry penguins with some very smelly pilchards; **Ben Brown**, for working tirelessly on my paddling technique; **Alexander Brylin**, the great Russian (Alex, one day I will come to eastern Russia and we will race down the Amur River together); **Brian Button**, the most inspiring swimming coach ever; **Jack Canfield**, for the wonderful times we've spent in Hawaii and for your wise counsel; **Victoria Cork**, for coordinating our rescue in the Indian Ocean; **Jonathan Deal**, for standing tall for the Karoo; **Melody Deas**, for taking beautiful photos in freezing conditions; **Professor Derry Devine**, for teaching me the Laws of the Sea and marine environmental law; **Dave Duarte**, for introducing me to the power and joy of social media; **Jonathan Dugas**, without whom we may never have discovered anticipatory thermo-genesis; **Lara Dugas**, for making very sure I did not get too thin; **Hendrik du Toit**, for being the first sponsor to write a cheque with my name on it; the Dane **Jonas Ellehauge**, for keeping a vigilant eye for hungry bears at Verlegenhuken; **Terje Eggum**, a superb photojournalist and a great Norwegian; **Kirsty Elliott**, for keeping the office running smoothly; the **English Channel Swimming Association**; **Andrew Evans**, one superb travel writer; **Dr Sean Gottschalk**, for overseeing the most dangerous swim; **Nozimasila Doris Giwu**, for looking after my family; **Ted Graham**, the legal eagle who kept me in the Thames and out of prison in the summer of 2006; my late cousin **Griff Griffiths**, for wonderful weekends in Brecon and Erwood;

Thanks

Bruno Giussani, who launched my speaking career (without knowing it!); **Sanjeev Gurung**, for looking after me on Mount Everest; **Professor John Hare**, the best kind of teacher; **Murad Hassan**, for showing us the beauty of the Maldives; **Róbert Hegedüs**, the great Hungarian athlete and a pretty special human being; **Michael Henderson**, school friend and lifeguard on Mount Everest; my father's cousin **Carey Hendrich** (No. 132 in the Great Escape), whose courage during the forced march of 1945 kept me going during Endurance; **Jørn Henriksen**, for driving the Zodiac in atrocious conditions; **Evelyn Holtzhausen**, for telling the truth about fracking; the **International Swimming Hall of Fame**; **Martin Jenkins**, for focusing me in the bus on the way to Nigards Glacier Lake and on Mount Everest; the **schoolchildren of Jostedal**, Norway, for cheering me on; my headmaster, the late **John Ince**, who did so much to make Camps Bay High School an inspiring place; **Clare Kerr**, for switching on the light; to **Peder Kjærvik**, for the warm shower (I will never forget it); **Motti Lewis**, for designing the cold-water training facilities at I&J, without which the polar swims would never have happened; **Emily Lewis-Brown**, for helping me better understand the science and for always supporting me; **Mahendra Singh Limbu**, for guiding me in the Himalayas and pointing out the butterflies; **Lt Col Crispin Lockhart** from the Ministry of Defence, for reviewing this book for any security issues; **Chris Lotz**, for the amazing scenes you captured; **Colonel**

Thanks

Vladimir Lutov, an officer and a gentleman, for helping make the World Winter Swimming Championships a joyful experience; **Stuart Makin**, for sound counsel; **John Mann**, for calling Roman; **Matthew Mansfield**, for giving me a second chance with the SAS; **Lord Marland**, for always being there for me; **Nic Marshall**, without whose enthusiasm and optimism we'd never have reached the North Sea; **James Mayhew**, who bravely fended off the swans in the Thames and whose skinny-dip in the Arctic shocked countless unsuspecting Africans; **Ben McGuire**, who swam me into Sydney Harbour; my kayaking doubles partner **Dawid Mocke**, long may we win races together; **Steven Munatones**, who has done so much for the sport of long-distance swimming; **Vladimir Nefatov**, for joining us in Oulu; **André Nel**, who introduced me to South Africa's townships and to whom I will always be indebted; **Marylin Noakes**, for inspiring us, especially the Prof; **Professor Tim Noakes**, for continually challenging beliefs and being so courageous at the North Pole; the **captain and crew of the MS *Nordstjernen***, who sailed us around Spitsbergen; **Donald Paul**, for helping me so much with that vital speech; **Georgie Pearce**, for being a font of good ideas; the **captain and crew of the yacht *Pelorus***; to **Nick Peterson**, a great SAS friend, companion at the North Cape, Sognefjord, Sydney and (hopefully!) my next expedition; **Alistair Petrie**, for psyching me up in the Real Cold War; the **captain and crew of the MV *Polar Star***, who sailed us across the Drake Passage four times;

Thanks

Stephen Praetorius, for future endeavours; **Mr Pretorius and his team at I&J**, for providing tons and tons of ice for our training; **Lucas Radebe**, for inspiration both on and off the field; **Binod Rai and his team of Sherpas**, the most professional guides in the Himalayas; **Jason Roberts**, for so much, but especially for volunteering to dive in and rescue me if anything went wrong at the North Pole; **Patsy Rodenburg**, an exceptional voice coach and a very special lady; **Margaret Roestorf** and the staff at SANCCOB, for protecting the most beautiful residents of the Cape; **Bronwen Rohland**, who supported me so much; **André van Rooyen** and **Sue Rutherford**, who designed our beautiful website; **Stephen Rubin**, whose generosity got us sailing; **Patrick Ryan**, for constant guidance; **Hugo Salamonsen**, whose encouragement got me around the North Cape; the **Sami reindeer herders** at North Cape – what a welcome sight you were; **Craig Scarpa**, for preparing me physically for Mount Everest; **Phurba Sherpa**, for carrying the kayak up the mountain and all the way down again; **Lucy Scott**, for cheering us under the bridges; **Tony Sellmeyer**, who helped me round the Cape of Good Hope and get a roof over my head; **Dr Damon Stanwell-Smith**, for ensuring that, however I die, it will not be because of some aggressive leopard seal (I can't think of a worse way to go!); all the members of **the public who swam sections of the Thames with me**; my friend and mentor **Dr Otto Thaning**, who showed me how to glide gracefully through

Thanks

the water; **Judy Tait** and the girls from Inanda Seminary, for connecting my heart with my voice; **Bardy Thomas**, a superb teacher; **Jenny Toyne Sewell**, for nursing all the malingerers; **General Tim Toyne Sewell**, for so much, but especially for leading the mutiny in the Indian Ocean – if you had not done it, God knows where we would be now; **Archbishop Desmond Tutu**, who inspired a nation and never fails to lead by example; **Tobie van Heerden**, for getting those flags to stand tall and strong along our route to the North Pole; **Jeremy Veniker**, for coaxing me metre by metre down that muddy river; **Michael Walker**, first to take a dip on Mount Everest and one heck of a photojournalist; my French teacher **Mr Weeks**, for inspiring us with stories of his travels in Africa; **Bruce Wigo**, for embracing sport with a purpose; **Graham Wilkinson**, from the Hampshire Flag Company, for always providing the most beautiful flags – an expedition is not an expedition without a good flag; my first headmaster, the late **Tony Wortham**, who made my childhood so happy and adventurous; **Richard Saul Wurman**, who made the call to TED; the **WWF** – keep up the great work; **President Ram Baran Yadav** of Nepal, who gave us such a generous reception despite the riots; the **captain, crew and polar bear guards of the I/B** *Yamal*; **Mariia Yrjö-Koskinen**, who put fun first at the World Winter Swimming Championships.

Thanks to the team that put this book together: **Jacqui L'Ange**, for your beautiful and thoughtful writing, and for

Thanks

your unswerving dedication to the project – it's been a joy to work with you; **Tessa Graham**, who helps me to put the expeditions together and make everything happen, and whose strategy is always bang on; project manager **Francine Blum**, for putting it all together; **Alfred LeMaitre**, for editing this book with a thoroughness I have never encountered before; **Valda Strauss** who completed the final edit while everyone else was enjoying the Easter holidays; **Anika Ebrahim**, for publicising the book like crazy; **Andrea Marchesi** for an amazing book tour; **Jeremy Boraine** and **Ingeborg Pelser**, for your support and for publishing this book in a tough market.

And heartfelt thanks to my family: my sister **Caroline**, my stepchildren **Taegyn** and **Finn**, and my ever-loving wife **Antoinette**, who is my pillar of support. Last, thanks to my mother, **Margery**, for sharing her love of geography and history and for reading many wonderful books to me as a child and to my late father **Patterson**, who filled me with self-belief and inspired me to dream.

Finally, thanks to the animals in my life, to **Nanu**, **Kanga** and **Lumi**, who bring constant joy, and to **the yaks** who got us onto Mount Everest and inspired me to write this book.

For more information on Lewis or to contact him,
visit lewispugh.com
or follow him on Facebook and Twitter (@LewisPugh)

Also available by Lewis Pugh
Achieving the Impossible
(Jonathan Ball Publishers)